CARPE DIEM

CARPE DIEM

a memoir

RIP MASON

This memoir is dedicated to my wonderful wife Diana and to our children Taylor, Charlotte, Colin and Kennedy, as well as to my goddaughter Maia.

Thank you all for the joy of life.

Contents

Be wise. Decant the wine, and since our time is brief, cut back your far-reaching hope. For even while we talk, envious time has fled. *Carpe diem*—seize the day, put little trust in the future.

~ *The Roman poet Horace, 23 BC*

Prologue

It was the longest of long shots.

My partners and I were hours from making our third-round and final bid in 1997 with a team at KKR, the premier private equity firm, to acquire Jafra Cosmetics International from Gillette. With no warning, I received a call at home from Perry Golkin, from KKR. We had been working for months to bring this together, and he was calling now to inform me that the firm had changed their plans and would not be submitting a bid with us the next morning.

My partners and I had spent hundreds of hours on the deal. We had traveled throughout Europe and Latin America. This extensive undertaking, involving the development of strategic plans and financial forecasts, was about to be lost in an instant.

If I still wanted to pull this off, I needed to find someone with hundreds of millions of dollars overnight.

As I hung up the phone and looked at the clock, only one option came to mind. I knew that Brian Finn, a former senior lender at Credit Suisse in New York, was Mary Kay's banker. Brian was well acquainted with direct-selling businesses like Jafra and its financings. He had recently left the bank and joined Clayton, Dubilier & Rice (CD&R), another New York–based private equity firm and competitor of KKR. I had never met Brian. I quickly called around to friends in financial circles and got Brian's home number. He answered, and I briefly explained the situation, noting that a final bid was required in just a few hours. I walked Brian through the financial metrics of the business and the proposed purchase as well as the deep and specialized experience of our management team.

This was a time when everyone was using fax machines. Brian had one at home, as did I. These machines made it possible to send documents to others instantly, but doing so meant hand-feeding each page. It took longer than an hour for me to send Brian our 100-page investment memo, much of which I had authored.

KKR was using the accounting firm of Deloitte for all its deal diligence. I assured Brian that the financial diligence was complete for bidding purposes, and if they were interested in the deal, I would call KKR to try to get access to their work product. Brian and I spoke for many hours that night—until well after 1:00 a.m. He had internal calls to make with his partners at CD&R, and we agreed to speak in an hour.

An hour later, my phone rang. "Rip, we are interested," Brian said. "This is a big ask at the final hour, but we will submit a $200 million bid on behalf of your team in the morning."

I will never forget this moment, not only because of the tension and drama of the last-minute save, but also because my involvement in the deal to purchase Jafra led to a turning point in my career—when I transitioned from being an attorney representing clients to becoming the head of a multinational corporation. Jafra was just the first of many.

This book is a gathering of stories from a journey spanning many decades. I have never kept a journal or diary, so the source material is my memories. Along the way, some exceptional people have believed in me and supported me.

My mom and dad provided abundant joy and encouragement. I miss them every day and give thanks for their love and generosity of spirit. My brother Tom and I have spent thousands of hours together hiking, skiing, laughing, and enjoying life. My sister Karen has always radiated joy and kindness to everyone, especially to me.

I know from reviewing these pages that I was provided with a number of unique opportunities. Travel has been an important element in my journey. I have walked the elegant streets of Paris, London, Munich, Rome, New York, and Tokyo, and I have been fortunate to work in each of these cities. I have also seen dire poverty in Darfur and Appalachia and violence in Baghdad.

Revisiting these stories has, at times, been an emotional encounter. It is balanced by the joy of abundant life, with much more to enjoy on the journey with my wife, children, and friends.

With all the travel I did professionally, it's not any wonder I had a number of encounters that involved amusing anecdotes. While most of these encounters were fleeting, I share several of them here.

Traveling alone across multiple time zones results in a curious array of passengers seated alongside me, often for ten hours or longer. I do not normally engage my seatmates, respecting the only quiet place remaining in this era of electronic encroachment. If a fellow traveler initiated a conversation, however, I always responded. Some of these seatmates included Carlos Santana, Barbara Walters, Robert Wagner, Gary Sinise, Tommy Lasorda, Marcus Allen, Kyra Sedgwick, John Legend, Nobu, George Takei, Kevin Kline, and Liza Minnelli.

In late 2000, during my Jafra years, I was flying from Los Angeles to London on British Airways, my preferred carrier, particularly for long journeys. I had flown British Air often enough that the ever-efficient BA staff greeted me in the first class sleeper cabin with a glass of Johnnie Walker Blue Label scotch, along with an assortment of cheeses, appetizers, and fresh fruit (a wonderful way to travel).

I always tried to get as much work out of the way as possible at the start of the flight before takeoff. The BA layout had a small desk next to each seat. I pulled a number of files from my briefcase and set to work. The first class cabin was arranged with one seat next to a window, two adjoining seats in the middle, and another single seat next to the window opposite. I was seated in one of the middle-row seats.

Focusing on my task and enjoying my cocktail, I sensed someone moving into the seat next to me. After a few moments, he inquired in a British accent, "Okay, what the hell do you do?"

Not missing a beat, I glanced over and responded, "Well, what the hell do you do? Oh, I know. You are that singer with one name...It's Sting, isn't it?"

We both laughed as he responded, "Yeah, I am that one-name singer...Sting. What are you drinking?"

We chatted for much of the night. His wife and child were seated in front of us, and he brought me up to meet them. They were on their way to London for Madonna's wedding to Guy Ritchie.

Approximately a year later, my business partner Ron Clark and I were having an early dinner at Toscana in Brentwood before we took that same overnight flight to London. We frequently had dinner before the flight to relax and visit favorite restaurants. We were the only diners in Toscana that night, and we sat comfortably at our table and ordered.

Suddenly, the door opened and in walked Julie Andrews and her husband Blake Edwards. Blake looked at me, smiled enthusiastically, walked over, and began pumping my hand in greeting.

"How are you?" he asked.

"Blake," I said. "I know who you are—and I really enjoyed your film 10—but I don't think I'm who you think I am."

He laughed and asked Mario, the manager, to seat them alongside Ron and me. A wonderful discussion with lots of laughter ensued. Julie was charming and told us stories about Blake, and we laughed the entire time. As we were getting the check, I mentioned to Julie, "You were so amazing on Broadway in Victor/Victoria. Do you remember, on opening night, when someone in the audience kept calling out, 'Julie, I love you!'"

"Was that you?" she exclaimed. "No, I wasn't there."

Blake roared with laughter, and Julie cracked up. A few moments later, I told her I did see the show shortly after it opened and loved it. In New York another special connection occurred, lasting but a few seconds. I was working very late and returned to the St. Regis hotel (my NY clubhouse) well after midnight. No one was in the lobby. The doorman greeted me and held the elevator. I walked into its tight confines and saw that standing right in front of me was Muhammad Ali. He was with his wife and an aide. I noticed he was trembling from Parkinson's disease.

In 1977, my brother and I, along with our great friend Doug Grau, scrimped and saved for the $75—a monumental amount at the time— we needed for the seats to see Ali fight Earnie Shavers at Madison Square Garden.

As the hotel elevator doors closed, I decided to do something contrary to my custom. I looked Ali in the eye, told him I had seen him fight Shavers, and thanked him for his career and courage, closing with, "You are indeed the greatest of all time."

He reached across and put his hand behind my head, pulling me toward him. We touched our foreheads for several seconds. As he released me, I saw a tear running down his wife's face. The elevator stopped, and the door opened. I stepped out. It was over in seconds but is a memory I will hold forever.

Chapter 1

Early Family Years

My brother and sister and I always looked forward to every Easter recess from grammar school for weeks in advance because it would be a great family adventure. Our parents packed us into the old station wagon in Princeton, and we made the long drive south to Florida, to Sanibel Island. This was a serious 24-hour trek for Dad, and he drove from one state to the next through the night.

Mom kept the three of us entertained by reading stories of pirates or American history and adventures. With three young kids crammed in the back seat, it was a family journey. Comfort was never a top consideration in the old car without air-conditioning careening through the southern states. We celebrated the crossing of state lines with a stop for a soda and a bathroom break.

Dad had read about Sanibel years earlier and learned it was a remote and undisturbed shelling paradise. He loved walking the quiet beaches and hunting for prized seashells. Each spring we went there, he taught us more about shells, and he developed an eye for the rarest of collectibles. This led to my brother, sister, and I scampering down the beach, gathering shells to show him.

In the summers, we piled into the station wagon (still no air-conditioning) and took off to the New Jersey shore. Folks from other places may know our state by the refineries along the New Jersey Turnpike, but generations from the area know the beauty, serenity, and sense of remoteness of New Jersey's beaches.

Great seafood. Swimming in the rolling waves until toes and fingers were puckered. Walks on the beach with my mother and father. Puzzles, family games playing Clue and Monopoly. There was no TV or radio. Definitely no phones. Dad with us all the time and not having to disappear every day to head to work. I remember this as a time when we were all together as a family.

I was also lucky to be a part of a large, close-knit family of grandparents, uncles and aunts, and cousins who celebrated differences and individual pursuits. The concept of family values is viable only for people who value their family and have faith in their loved ones. Running away from family gatherings was an alien idea to me. I always looked forward to family retreats like they were a special holiday.

My wife Diana likes to say that I grew up in a Norman Rockwell family. My dad was an attorney and a dedicated family man, who was also involved in numerous charitable organizations, including the YMCA and United Way. He was born on Hamilton Avenue in Trenton, NJ, and his father was an engineer at Texaco.

Dad attended Trenton Central High School and graduated from Princeton University in 1936. He waited tables through his years at Princeton to pay his tuition. He received his law degree from the University of Pennsylvania in 1939 and shortly after was admitted to the New Jersey State Bar.

He was just beginning his legal career when the Japanese bombed Pearl Harbor on December 7, 1941, and shortly after that the United States entered World War II. He and other young men of that time must have been anticipating this, and Dad enlisted shortly after war was declared, joining the army. He was stationed in the Pacific, and even served for a time on General Douglas MacArthur's staff.

Like many of his generation, my father rarely talked about the bleak realities of the war. Instead, he delighted us with stories about the exotic islands, beaches, and fishing. He always said he was lucky the army sent him to Hawaii, Guam, and Tahiti. At the end of the war, Dad was stationed in Bora-Bora, where he was a captain. I suspect the realities of the war, even in such a beautiful place, were far less entertaining than he portrayed them.

Back home after the Allied victory, Dad was able to resume his law practice, and that's how he met my mom in the late 1940s. Jean Harris was a graduate of Princeton High School, and she attended the Katharine Gibbs secretarial school in New York City, where she learned to be a blazing typist. She started working in Dad's law office, and at first their connection was just professional and then it became more than that. She was 13 years younger than Dad, and they were married in September 1950. I was born in August 1951, just before midnight, which meant I missed having the same birthday as my mom's dad by only two minutes.

My father's side of my family was small and organized, akin to a filing cabinet. He had two siblings, a brother and sister. Uncle Fred was known as Bucket, and I never learned how he got that nickname, even though our families spent a great deal of time hanging out together over the years. Uncle Fred and Aunt Mary had two kids, Daniel, who was known as Danny and was born the same year I was, and David.

Aunt Peg was my dad's sister and the youngest in the family. My father wrote letters to her weekly while he was away during the war, sharing his own tales of the Pacific. The tenderness and affection of his writing demonstrated the deep love, constant oversight, and encouragement of an older brother. Aunt Peg married Don Marcks, who had one of the most entertaining personalities I had come across in my young life. Uncle Don was always the one who entertained us with funny stories and abundant laughter. He had a booming voice that resounded and intervened in every corner of the room.

Like my dad, Uncle Don fought with the Allies during World War II. He was a bomber pilot who flew in the skies over Europe. One day he was scratched from a mission due to illness, and the plane he would have been flying was shot down and the entire crew was lost.

I learned when I was in my late teens that my father had another sister who passed away when she was very young. I'm sure that the family was devastated.

Our family had two farms my dad owned in central New Jersey. One was in Hopewell, and the other, closer by, was in Harbourton, and this was where most of our family gatherings were held. They were exciting and much-anticipated events and so many memories of the whole family gathered together during my formative years took place there. A typical weekend at the farmhouse included three-legged races, water balloon fights, and family softball games. Over the years, I became attached to the farm's ambiance and soft touches. I was determined that one day I would make it my home. If the family wasn't at the farm, we still gathered for Spaghetti Sundays—no one dared miss Uncle Don's sauce—at our home in Princeton or at my cousins' home in Ewing. These were treasured family events.

Aunt Peg and Uncle Don had five kids, and adding those cousins to the two from the Bucket Mason household and the three from ours, we made a clique of ten rowdy youngsters. We were regularly joined in our games by our aunts, uncles, and grandparents. My partner in crime in those early years—and for the rest of our lives—was my cousin Jeff, who was born only three weeks apart from me. We have been inseparable from childhood until this day. We did everything together, from going to summer camp and skiing to partying late at night.

Before I was old enough to start going away to summer camp, we spent most weekends and summers at the Harbourton farm and at the Jersey Shore. A typical scene from those nights was of my dad standing on the lush grass of our lawn, behind a grill, cooking hot dogs and burgers. I recall sitting on a tractor with my dad as we rode around cutting that grass. His shorts were smeared with meat juices and sauce-dipped handprints that we had left behind while chasing around, trying to catch lightning bugs with Mom.

A story from our young years at the Jersey Shore involves my sister Karen. One afternoon Tom, Dad, and I were slapping around in the surf when we heard Mom shouting. Soon the lifeguard whistles were blowing, and everyone was ordered out of the turbulent water. Karen was missing. There was a happy ending of the saga following some tense minutes. I'm sure Mom and Dad were near panic. The men joined hands along the beach and headed as one into the water, while Mom tried to stay calm between bursts of tears, her fist in her mouth to stop herself from screaming.

Dad asked me to run back and check the house. In moments, I was across the sand, running the 50 yards or so to the house. It was silent as I entered. I looked in the bathrooms. Nothing. Finally, I went to the bedroom where the three of us had our beds. Karen was fast asleep in her bed—still in her wet bathing suit covered with sand, which now covered her pillow. She was so peaceful I didn't want to wake her.

I ran back to the beach, waving for Mom and Dad and shouting, "I found her." From that day on, if we couldn't find Karen, everyone always asked, "Is she napping?"

As a kid, I never really knew what my father did for work, though I knew his job was corporate and he wore crisp white shirts, suits, and matching ties. I came to understand that he was involved with leaders of finance and industry. Still, to us, he was just Dad. He was our comfort place, and he always knew what to say to encourage us. He was always smiling and extending his kindness to people around him without expecting anything in return. He and Mom always had a kind word of encouragement.

My dad was also my first and best teacher, especially when it came to knowing what was the right way to be in the world. On one of those spring drives to Florida in the late 1950s, I remember being at a rest stop in Georgia. This was one of our traditional state line breaks, and I headed to the bathroom. I was just learning to read. Dad was standing with the gas station attendant, who was filling the tank. As I looked at the doors of the restroom, one said "Colored Only." The other door said "Men."

Karen, Tom (in Mom's arms), Mom and Rip Jersey Shore. 1955

I returned to the car and pulled on Dad's sleeve, asking which door I should use.

He bent down and put his hand on my shoulder. "Use that one, son," he said, pointing to the "Colored Only" door.

This was a lesson I carried forward throughout life.

When the families gathered, the cousins seemed to talk well into the night, not caring about time and space. On many occasions, we ended up on the floor in laughing fits. I remember the pain knots in our guts and watery eyes from laughing so hard. We were great friends, but we also took our games and the competition seriously, even during playful matches of dirtball, snowball, or rock fights. Creativity came to us naturally. We developed often-complicated self-serving rules and dangerous games to keep our bustling energy at bay.

One of our most absurd ventures among the boys involved all of us standing in line against the basement walls and turning off the lights. We then raced to the center of the room and collided with one another. We ended up with a few bloody noses, banged-up knees, and an occasional black eye. To keep from being scolded by Dad or Uncle Don for our reckless behavior, we made the younger cousins bite their tongues and endure the pain. We hurled strong phrases like "pain maketh a man" at them so we could avoid trouble. We really had a way of spinning situations in our favor. Luckily no one ever got really hurt, and we jumped back on our feet, laughing at one another, tripping silly and relishing everyone's infectious laughter.

That was my dad's side of the family, but I also had my mom's brother Uncle Tim and his wife Aunt Bette. They and their four kids were a key part of my life growing up. For me, Tim was the embodiment of an American man. He did everything you would expect an American male to do, like excelling at sports. I remember going with my mother to her younger brother's softball games at Marquand Park in Princeton, when I was not more than six years old. Whenever he was on the field, the crowd went wild, and the uproar was deafening when a ball he hit went outside the park and over Route 206. When I was a teenager, I played on that field for several years, but I was never able to land that kind of shot. It was truly remarkable.

Starting when I was six years old, I went to summer camp every year in Blairstown, NJ, at what was known at the time as Central New Jersey YMCA camps. A few years later, the camp was renamed after my dad as YMCA Camp Ralph S. Mason. It was a tribute to Dad, who founded the camp following the loss of its predecessor, Camp Wilson, during a flood on the Delaware River in 1955. During his years at Princeton University, my dad was a camp counselor at Wilson, and that's when he developed his love for the outdoors and giving back to others.

One of my earliest childhood memories was the first time we made the long drive to visit Blairstown. Dad was looking for a new site for the camp, and the place that would become the camp was just a farm with cows and a large pond. It was a hot summer day, and the sun was centered in the sky like a yolk in a sunny-side up egg. Its beams were scorching our skin. The pond called to us, and before we knew it, we were heading out to jump in and go skinny-dipping.

That spot became YMCA Camp Ralph Mason, and I enjoyed life as a camper there from the summer I was six years old until I was 17 years old. My cousins went there as well, and the experience was like an extension of our family times at the farm in Harbourton. My favorites over the years were riflery, hiking, canoeing, and swimming, and as each summer ended, I started counting the days until we could go back the next summer.

The camp was so important to all of us that decades later, my brother Tom and his wife Emily, who are accomplished bike riders, initiated an annual bike ride fundraiser to help keep the camp going. (Tom was then the chairman of the camp's board of trustees.) The participants departed from Tom and Emily's Hopewell farm for a 70-plus-mile ride finishing at the camp. There, a few hundred campers and staff lined the road that led to the camp entrance. They cheered and shouted words of encouragement to the bikers.

Every year Tom and Emily designed world-class biking kits that included custom shirts of the finest quality with sponsor logos on the front and back. The shoulder of each shirt had a daffodil, my mom's favorite flower. In later years, I tried to make the event as grand as possible and got the companies I ran to lend their support, and I also invited many generous friends to make sponsor donations.

Our family was entwined with the larger community in Princeton, and we became a part of it. Princeton Hospital became our personal baby-retrieving depot. My mother and Uncle Tim were born there, and my mother gave birth to me there, followed by my brother Tom and my sister Karen. Many years later, my kids Charlotte and Taylor opened their eyes in the same hospital. As a kid, I attended Princeton public schools, the same schools where my mother and Uncle Tim went. A number of the teachers who taught my mother in grammar school were amazingly still teaching when I attended. By the time I ended sixth grade, my mother and I had had four of these same teachers. Mrs. Forsyth, my kindergarten teacher, taught my mother at the start of her career then taught me at the end of her career. Things came full circle.

My elementary school years in Princeton felt like growing up in a small town. My friends and I roamed around the town in packs, riding our bikes with no helmets. We were gone for hours and returned home only in time for dinner. We loved riding on a gust of wind, promising us a new adventure every day. We were aspiring explorers ready to leave our mark on the town's map. Our freedom allowed us to pedal through unlikely places without a sense of dread and danger. We often rode into town and. across the university campus to visit my grandfather, Leigh Harris, who played a prominent role for many years at the Palmer Physical Laboratory at Princeton. Everyone in the family called him Pappy, and whenever he saw me, he always stopped whatever he was doing and welcomed me into his warm embrace with contagious laughter. His eyes lit up like a wizard whose audience had just arrived. He entertained me and my friends by showing us the glass wonders he crafted for the scientists at the lab. They twinkled in the light like a northern star in the sky.

Years later, my sister was looking at a photograph in a book about Albert Einstein, who spent many of his later years also at the Palmer labs and who was a colleague of my grandfather's, and she recognized a bud vase that Pappy had made for him. Einstein was proudly displaying the vase in his living room like a prized possession. I have a duplicate of that vase.

Dad World War II. 1945

Pappy was my mother's dad, and he played an influential role in my life. He and my grandmother, known as Bamma, were originally from Schenectady in upstate New York. Pappy grew up on a farm and had eight brothers and sisters. Big family meant familial love was abundant, and I believe that is how the spirit of togetherness pooled in the following generations. Pappy and three of his brothers went off together to Europe to fight in World War I. All four returned after seeing the atrocities of war and destruction, each nursing their own traumas and drowning in the torment of their own experiences.

The brothers survived the horrors of gas attacks and machine-gun charges into enemy lines. One of them, Uncle Ray, returned home with the loss of an eye. I often asked Pappy about the war, but he was reluctant to discuss it. One afternoon, when I was a teenager, we were relaxing on the lawn together and enjoying the summer warmth and smell of fresh-cut grass. He told me about a time he was in a trench with a German soldier. I sensed his sadness as he described retrieving the soldier's papers and personal items. Many years later, it occurred to me that Pappy had left out part of the story, and the soldier was alive with him in the trench. It was likely they fought, ultimately resulting in the death of the young German. I know Pappy was devastated by seeing the photos of the young man with his friends and family.

Pappy received medals for his service from the United States, France, and Belgium. Like my father and his time during World War II, Pappy did not like to talk about the war, and I don't think many people who sang his praises about his work and community activism even knew he'd been a soldier. Pappy was a gentle soul and had an immense love of his family—qualities he maintained, even though during his youth he was pushed into an experience that marred his innocence. His kindness was so much a part of his existence that even animals could sense it.

In their later years, my grandparents lived on a farm that my dad bought for them. I saw deer walk up to Pappy uninvited and eat pears from his hand. He sat on the front porch, and squirrels stood on his chest to snatch peanuts from his mouth. Chickadees landed on his open hand to peck at sunflower seeds. It was hard to imagine a man like him standing on the battlefield holding a rifle or doing anything remotely harmful. He embodied kindness and gentleness.

Pappy returned from the war to Schenectady and attended glassblowing classes at the Corning glassworks. I never thought to ask why he decided to pursue this, but it put him in a good position to make a next career move. He saw that Princeton University was advertising for a glassblower in the physics department, and he recognized it as a once-in-a-lifetime kind of opportunity. Princeton was as renowned then as it is today, and Pappy and Bamma headed to New Jersey for an interview. Pappy had the right credentials, and he was told he would get the job if he could successfully create a glass fusion pump. No one had successfully built one before, and they needed 20 of them in 30 days.

Many years later—over a cold beer with much laughter—Pappy and Bamma described the next 30 days. Pappy never left the lab and didn't accept any visitors. He made it his fortress. Bamma brought him all his meals, and she set up a cot along the wall so he could rest without leaving. After numerous attempts and several close calls, he finally succeeded in creating the first pump on day 25. Over the next five days, largely without any sleep, he completed the order and built 19 more.

When he showed up with his creations, the chiefs in the physics department were floored. His achievement was exceptional enough to merit applause from the experts in the field. He was an instant celebrity, and everyone appreciated what he had done. Needless to say, he also got the job, and he and Bamma moved to Princeton and that's how my mom's family ended up in the area.

Palmer Physical Laboratory at Princeton University and later the Institute for Advanced Study were on the cutting edge of the new movement in physics and engineering. Over the next half century, Pappy worked with many notables there, including Albert Einstein and Robert Oppenheimer, who later led the Manhattan Project in the development of the atomic bomb. My mom enjoyed telling stories over dinner, and she entertained us all with one about taking me up to Palmer labs to have lunch with Pappy. According to her story, Einstein, the greatest physicist of every era, was there, and apparently, he was fond of young children. Per family lore, Einstein rubbed my head and, in his heavy German accent, proclaimed, "What a beautiful boy!"

Leigh Harris ("Pappy") - Palmer Physics Laboratory, Princeton University. 1958

I had to get my head around that story. My mom liked telling it, and my dad laughed and repeated Einstein's pronouncement in his improvised heavy German accent. That caused everyone at the dining room table to break into hilarious laughter and do their own version of, "What a beautiful boy!"

I grew up thinking that every family was like mine—loving, kind, and understanding. Only many years later, I discovered this wasn't so, and that it was a privilege to have a family this joyous, unique, and supportive. We never had to worry about angry outbursts and raised voices—unless of course Karen, Tom, and I were stuck in the back seat of a car for 24 hours, which happened during our long car rides to Florida for spring vacation.

Watching the Olympics in 1964 when I was 12 years old spurred new aspirations in my young heart as I decided I would learn how to ski. My preteen self could not think of a more perfect winter activity. On the next Christmas Eve, Dad drove me down to Korvettes in Trenton during a blinding snowstorm. He helped me pick out my first skis. They were wooden and sleek to the touch and came with cable bindings and leather lace-up boots. My cousin Jeff and I started skiing together at Belle Mountain. I'm not sure why it was called that—there isn't a mountain, rather just a small hill. It was a ski run with a rope tow on the Delaware River. But no matter, I was hooked and could not believe I'd been missing the fun all along. This was the beginning of many years of skiing in my future.

For junior high, I went to Valley Road School, the same school that my mom and Uncle Tim attended. I was enrolled in the Hun School of Princeton for my high school academics. From the moment I stepped foot on the Hun school premises, I was mystified by its environment. It was a prep school in the literal sense, all boys and in the English tradition. The school uniform was jackets and ties, and we had classes six days a week, a practice today's generation can't even comprehend. The school operated on a set of strict rules, and violators could easily be suspended or expelled. They really kept us in line, a practice that continues today. My daughter Kennedy is a senior there now, and she has embarrassingly excellent grades. She is also one of a few basketball players in the school's history to have scored 1,000 points in a season. No matter how many times I protested that she was making my record look bad, I was never expecting her to dull her shine for my sake. She is meant for the sky.

My dad was on the Hun board of trustees, and when he stepped down after more than 30 years, I was honored to be appointed in his place. In recognition of my father's tenure, the headmaster's house on campus was named Mason House. I served on the Hun board for ten years, including nine as chairman, starting at age 34 and stepping down in 1999.

Princeton was a small town so coming across familiar faces at every corner was not a rare occurrence. Uncle Tim was a Hun math teacher and also my JV football coach. My focus was sports and academics back then. In junior year, I was elected vice president of the day students. I continued to serve in the student council and was elected as the president for my senior year. I started playing football at Hun as a sophomore, and that's when I met Skitch Donald. My friendship with Skitch was unbreakable during our high school years.

Skitch had a quiet and confident personality that was hard to miss in a room full of teenagers. He pulled into my driveway every morning in his smelly blue VW Bug to give me a ride to school. He was also over to our house for dinner several nights a week, even though we never really extended an official invitation. Everyone in the house expected Skitch to be at our doorstep when the clock struck 6:00 p.m. He was always on time and never failed to entertain us all.

Dad would hear him outside and shout, "Come in, Skitch!" without even asking who was at the door. Eventually, he stopped attempting to knock and strolled into the house like he was part of the family. My friends and I were in and out of one another's homes all the time in those days. I ate at Skitch's house many nights too. He also stayed in our basement sometimes during the week. Sometimes, two or three friends from the Hun football team joined Skitch after the practice, and we all enjoyed a night filled with laughter, delicious food, and enthusiastic cheer.

My mom was always prepared to feed all these guys who gathered at our house. She was already feeding two growing sons of her own. I bet Tom and I ate five times a day if you counted three main meals and eating in between. I was always trying to gain weight for football, which I really loved. I was a wide receiver, and I had to be fast. Good thing I was able to outrun so many of the guys who were bigger than me. I enjoyed football and hockey, but I wanted to be the best, and that required physical size.

Fortunately, the Hun football team was undefeated in my junior and senior years. We maintained a streak of 31 wins, an impressive record that stands its ground in New Jersey high school records to this day.

Hun School Princeton, NJ. 1969

During my high school years, the country was undergoing tremendous upheaval and change. The civil rights movement, which began in the 1950s, hit its peak in the early 1960s with the passage of the Civil Rights Act and the Voting Rights Act. At the same time, America was increasing its involvement in the war in Vietnam, causing protests to erupt, especially in the coastal states and on university campuses. In 1968, I was a high school junior, and that year saw a tidal wave of events I couldn't ignore. Martin Luther King Jr. was assassinated in Memphis, TN, and riots broke out in more than 100 cities. During a presidential election headed for November, Senator Robert Kennedy, the clear favorite among the country's youth, was assassinated after winning the California primary. The Chicago police attacked demonstrators outside the Democratic convention two months later. Images of the attack sickened the nation.

I already had an interest in history and politics, and when I became a senior in fall 1968, I enrolled in a political science class taught by George Warren, an exceptional and motivational teacher. He was larger than life, with a booming voice and an incredible depth of knowledge concerning history and politics. Warren reviewed the issues of the day in an evenhanded and a balanced way, encouraging open debate and discussion. This was the year when we were deciding where we wanted to go to college, and I had determined I wanted to pursue a political science degree.

I knew what a college should look like and feel like from having grown up near Princeton with my dad's and grandfather's close associations with the university. My love of skiing focused me on New England schools with good political science programs and close proximity to the slopes. That way I could pursue both the intellectual and physical. One of our neighbors who had attended Middlebury College in Vermont told me great things about it. The first time I saw the campus, I knew that it was my first choice, and I was thrilled when I was accepted there in the spring of my senior year in high school, to begin that fall.

The rest of my senior year was relaxed. My grades were good, life at home was as exciting as ever, and the Jersey Shore was just a drive away for my friends and me. I was enjoying the best days of my life. One morning after we'd all gotten our acceptances to colleges, I was told I had to take the ACT biology exam. I thought all the standardized testing was behind me but apparently not. I was not intimidated by these exams, but I did think the task seemed frivolous. Still, somewhere in the deepest parts of my consciousness, I had been dreading this biology test. Science was not my strong suit, and I had not taken a biology class since sophomore year. Skitch was told he had to take the ACT chemistry exam. We were determined we knew how to approach this and never lost our bearing.

When the test day arrived, we thought it made perfect sense to go out for lunch and a cold beer since we were only one or two months away from graduation. We arrived back at school after breath mints and gum had eliminated the beer evidence on our breath. We were relaxed and in a good mood for the exam—without a shred of tension. It is surprising what wonders a glass of beer can do for your mood. The test booklets were handed out upside down in the well-rehearsed, standardized-test protocol. The instructor announced "begin" after clocking the start of the exam. The tension among the other students was palpable as they nervously tapped their feet and murmured under their breath.

Meanwhile, I coursed through my exam, leafing through the folds of memory to pick apart schoolwork from two years earlier. In the first inning, in what would become an interesting testing phenomenon over the next several years, I finished the two-hour test in less than one hour. I did not believe the clock and figured I must have missed a section and went through the test booklet a second time. No sections were missed. I redid the whole exam to see if I could catch any mistakes, but everything was accurate as per memory.

There were still 30 minutes left on the clock, and I was getting anxious. I waited for someone else to finish before me so I could turn in my exam. Finally, a kid I did not recognize finished five minutes before the exam time. I was out of my seat in an instant, turned in my test, and left the examination hall.

A month later, I was walking through the Hun hallways when I heard an announcement over the school PA system, "Rip Mason, report to Mr. Bing's office."

Sandy Bing was the dean of students, and it was never good being called to his office. I wracked my brain to figure out what I could have possibly done wrong. Nada—so I put on my meekest and most pitiful face as I walked into the dean's office. That's when I saw two men in suits sitting in front of Mr. Bing.

"We are here to ask you about the biology ACT," one of the men said.

Those words were enough to throw my brain into a panicked frenzy. I thought maybe they had figured out that I had had a beer before the exam.

"You had a perfect test score," he said.

I exhaled and almost hit the ground as relief flooded through my nerves. Next the man asked if I might be interested in pursuing a science degree rather than liberal arts.

I was flattered but saw my performance on the test as a one-off episode and did not end up pursuing a career in science. Crisis averted.

Chapter 2

Middlebury, Africa 1973

My parents drove me up from Princeton to Middlebury in late summer 1969 for freshman orientation and the start of classes. I recall feeling expectant, but I wasn't anxious. Mom and Dad may have been going through a variety of emotions. Years later when I took my son Taylor to Syracuse University to start college, I appreciated that parental sense of separation my parents must have gone through that day with me.

I was given my dorm room assignment, which indicated that I would spend my first year in Stewart Hall with roommate Charles Cavness, who was from Colorado. Dad helped me haul my trunk and ski equipment up the flights of stairs, and we found the room. I could tell that Charles had already arrived, but there were no suitcases or clothes in the closet. The only things he had moved in were an orange backpack and climbing rope, both sitting on his bed.

Mom and Dad helped me unpack and as they were getting ready to leave, Charles arrived and greeted us. That's when we learned that his possessions had been shipped from Denver and would arrive in several weeks.

I walked my mother and father out to the car to say goodbye. Many years later, Dad recounted what happened in the car as they were pulling away. Mom was teary-eyed as they were waving goodbye. Dad recalled telling Mom, "Don't look back. He's on his own now."

Being paired with Charles (later called Charlie, and occasionally Chuck, in a form of derision) as my freshman roommate was the beginning of a lifelong adventure. Over the years we skied in the winter months at the Middlebury College Snow Bowl, and he invited me to Colorado to visit his family on Christmas break. We skied in Aspen, Vail, and other legendary Colorado resorts. In those years, Aspen and Vail were small towns—not the bustling, chic destinations they are today. I remember my first week of classes at Middlebury as an awakening. I had always been on the honor roll, head of student government, a decent athlete, and a great student at the Hun School in Princeton. At Middlebury I was surrounded every day by all-star, highly motivated students, and it was intimidating to try to stand out among such exceptional peers. In addition, I was struck by how much more classwork and preparation was required. Hun prided itself on being a rigorous institution. This was on another level. Fortunately, the abundant reading and writing required at Hun had prepared me to amp my efforts and churn through the vast assignments as an entering freshman.

I have often described those first months at Middlebury, leading up to the Thanksgiving holiday, as the psychological midpoint of my college career. It was a period of intellectual adjustment and challenge, but it was also full of great wonder and exploration.

Colorado was far for Charlie to travel for Thanksgiving, and I invited him to join me and travel to Princeton. My mom put on the traditional dinner—with a big gathering of aunts and uncles and cousins in attendance. This was the first of many Thanksgivings Charlie spent with us, and he soon became a part of the family.

My last exam as a freshman turned out to be a repeat of the surprising ACT test I had taken a year earlier at Hun. All freshman at Middlebury were required to take a science course. I took geology in the fall—it was affectionately referred to as "Rocks for Jocks." For the spring semester, freshmen geology students were placed in an oceanography class taught by world-famous scientist David Folger. He later directed the Atlantic Marine Geology branch of the U.S.

Geologic Survey of the Woods Hole Oceanographic Institution in Massachusetts. The other students in the class were dedicated science majors, and I was an average student.

Rip Middlebury College. 1973

My goal was to end the year with a solid grade average, and as the oceanography final exam approached, I studied with intention and determination. Two hours were scheduled to take the test, and I plowed through the questions and completed them in 40 minutes. A sense of panic overwhelmed me. Had I missed a section or completely misunderstood a major question? I went through the exam a second time. Nothing was missing. I sat there forlorn, accepting my fate that my grade point average would deteriorate because of a low score on the test. Finally, near the two-hour mark, another student got up and put their exam booklet on the desk. I meekly did the same.

That summer I was at Camp Highlander, and one evening an announcement over the loudspeaker said I should come to the camp office. My dad was on the phone.

"I have some great news, son," he said. "You're on the dean's list, and you made an A on your oceanography final."

Deep exhale.

In the late spring of 1969, as I was ending my senior year in high school, Uncle Tim called and asked me if I wanted to run the riflery program at Camp Highlander in North Carolina, where he was the camp director. Until then, I had spent my summers at Camp Mason and thought I would end up spending my college summers there.

Uncle Tim knew about my success in the sport of competitive shooting, starting when I was in grammar school. My dad built a range for me in our basement. I came home from school and sports every night and practiced. My father drove me to meets around the Northeast, where I competed with others my age. It was a great opportunity for us to spend time together. I continued with the sport into my college years and excelled at it. I wanted to be successful. As I progressed in the sport, I won a number of state championships.

I accepted Uncle Tim's offer to run the program and take advantage of the skills I had learned. I was on my way to the Great Smoky Mountains in the western corner of North Carolina. The camp was owned by the Pine Crest School, a private school in Fort Lauderdale, FL, where Uncle Tim was a dean. I was the only camp staff member from the Northeast, and I found myself among a group of exceptional and dedicated counselors. Most of the campers were from Florida and came from broken homes with parents who had divorced. For many of them, this month away at camp was the closest sense of family they would enjoy during their grammar school and middle school years.

Camp Highlander was all about the kids and exposing them to an immersive outdoor adventure. The camp was perched on top of a mountain, and as a result the facilities were limited, and it did not have a swimming pool. Instead of traditional camp sports and competitions, there was hiking and rock climbing. Wonderful bonds were formed as kids that had been raised in luxury were sleeping outdoors without access to electronics and comforts of home.

My uncle let me design and implement the rifle program in the way I thought was best. I had a modest budget, and I reached out to some rifle supply shops that had supported me in New Jersey to help us upgrade and modify the equipment. The kids were a joy to work with. They sucked up my instruction, and I quickly assembled and trained a group of dedicated and highly qualified shooters. It would have been great to have matches with other camps, but they were too far away. Instead, I contacted the NRA and enrolled the top shooters as a team for the national summer camp Postal Matches. The NRA mailed targets to hundreds of camps with a quick deadline for sending back the completed targets. Uncle Tim and I, along with the kids and all the camp staff, were thrilled when my team finished number two in the United States during our second season.

My greatest lesson from the experience with these campers and my takeaway from these years was discovering my instinct and ability to teach. Later in my professional career those lessons and methods served me well running my own law firm and finally in the operation of large companies. The dedication and practice needed to excel in riflery instilled in me a work ethic and confidence that would be critically important to my legal and business operational success.

I vividly remember the emotion as the children departed at the end of each camp season. The staff, who stayed an extra day, left with tears and promises to return the next year. Summer camps often experience a significant staff turnover from year to year, but during my five years at Highlander, nearly every counselor returned each year. The emotional connections between us have lasted a lifetime. Later in my life and career, as I became engaged in direct sales, I experienced that dual sense of fulfillment and sadness as a season came to a close.

In 1964, Pappy retired from the physics department at Princeton, and the university had arranged a surprise tribute and retirement reception for him. This had to be kept from all the grandchildren too because none of us could keep a secret. Uncle Tim, Aunt Bette, and their kids were living in Florida, and they were driving up to surprise Pappy at the party. It was an exciting time as we tried to hush our voices and whisper warnings in one another's ears.

Pappy did not expect any of it. Seeing his face when he walked into the room, and seeing it glowing again was the best moment ever. His happiness was reaching out to us in waves.

Robert Goheen, the Princeton University president, gave a wonderful speech in which he recounted Pappy's numerous accomplishments. Many of the physics professors who knew his work also spoke. It was an overwhelming testament to his impact throughout the university community. They presented him with a book made up of letters of gratitude from former students. Among these were letters from several Nobel Prize recipients. Pappy accepted it all gracefully and was touched at the outpouring of thanks. The grandchildren, including me, were in awe of the achievements by this kind and gentle man. Several years later, after Pappy was no longer with us, we learned that during World War II, he participated in the Manhattan Project to develop the atomic bomb. He made frequent trips to Oak Ridge, TN, sometimes for several months at a time. Oak Ridge was the first and largest of the three Manhattan Project facilities. It was built in 1942 and was home to the uranium enrichment plant. The gas diffusion technology that Pappy first developed in the Palmer lab was essential to these efforts. During the war, the US intelligence services were engaged in a race against time with the Germans, who were also thought to be developing an atomic weapon.

One can imagine how daunting it was for Pappy and his colleagues to know the lives of millions were dependent on them succeeding at their work. He was a part of history and played an important role in events that defined the fate of many nations in the coming years.

During my freshman year at Middlebury, at a time when we were all more careful about long-distance phone calls, I telephoned my parents every Sunday evening. Following that call, I called Bamma and Pappy every week and told them about my life in Vermont. They were aware of every small and big incident that happened in my life.

The summer of 1971, between my sophomore and junior college years, I was working at Camp Highlander, where Uncle Tim was the camp director and my boss. My cousin Leigh and I lived in a small shack along with our friend Bob Clampett, the head of the waterfront activities.

Late one night, I was tucked into my sleeping bag, getting some rest after a tiring day. Suddenly the silence was broken by the sound of my Aunt Bette yelling for me. She burst into our cabin, with tears in her eyes. She had just learned that Pappy had died.

This was devastating for all of us, and the events following his death tired us out emotionally. My mom and her dad were exceptionally close, and his abrupt heart attack and death were emotionally scarring for her for the balance of her life. She was a strong and happy woman, but remembering the loss of her father would bring tears, especially at the holidays because Pappy represented the true spirit of Christmas. In one moment, I had lost my first mentor. We took solace knowing that Pappy's work would be part of people's memories forever. Today, there is a permanent display honoring his work at the Princeton University physics lab.

The late 1960s and early 1970s were a time of turmoil in America and especially for students on university campuses. Most of us had grown up in homes that admired and respected life in the United States. Many of us were the sons and daughters of veterans.

Vietnam was a turning point for American students. It was the first war broadcast live on television, and the daily reports of soldiers killed were sickening. Everyone seemed to know someone or had a friend who was serving in the American military half a world away.

We could not understand or process the reasons for their sacrifice. Peaceful protests emerged across the country and on university campuses.

In the weeks before I left home to go to Middlebury, on my 18th birthday in August 1969, Skitch and I drove down to Trenton, to the Selective Service office, which was better known as the draft board. All males who were 18 years old were required to register by completing the forms, and a few weeks later I received my draft card. I had noted in the registration form that in September I was attending Middlebury, and so I was issued the standard 2-S college student deferment. Activists across the country protested the unfairness of affluent guys who could afford to attend universities and avoid service in Vietnam, while predominantly poor young men were drafted.

That November the Selective Service Act was amended. Student deferments ended, and service would be based on an annual lottery. Every male over age 18 was eligible to be drafted. Everyone was very anxious as the first draft lottery drawing was televised nationally on December 1, 1969. Balls representing every day of the year were placed into a bin and picked out randomly. An early lottery number based on the date of birth assured that you were heading to Vietnam. I recall watching this with friends, many of whom were a year or two older and therefore eligible for the draft. Early selections were met with outbursts of emotion. In subsequent months we learned that only numbers drawn 195 or higher would not be drafted.

I was eligible the second year of the lottery, when I was 19 years old. My student deferment was canceled the prior year. The lottery was held on July 1, and I was working at Camp Highlander. I listened to the selection of the birthdays on the radio, and I was stunned to hear my number pulled among the first 50 selections. I called my dad. His law partner Hervey Moore was a colonel in the National Guard. Hervey said the Selective Service had called more draftees than needed. He assured us that there would not be another call-up until November.

I continued in my fall term, finding it difficult to concentrate on my studies as November approached. The call-up finally arrived and the draft notices did not reach my number for selection. Throughout this time, students were protesting the country's involvement in Vietnam on university campuses everywhere, and unexpectedly, President Nixon declared a draft holiday for the Christmas season. I had made it to January 1, 1971, without being drafted, which meant I satisfied the Selective Service rules for a year of eligibility, placing me automatically in second-priority status. All 365 birthdays in 1951 would have to be called up before they could reach mine. My chances of being drafted were slim.

Near the end of my freshman year at Middlebury, on May 4, 1970, four unarmed Kent State University students who were protesting against the war were shot and killed by Ohio National Guard troops. Nine other students were injured, one of whom was left paralyzed. This shocked the nation, and within hours of the shooting, more than four million university students joined protests in outrage. Classes were canceled at Middlebury and other campuses.

That evening I joined other students, faculty, and administrators for a packed gathering at Mead Chapel on our campus. Any student or faculty member could go to the front of the chapel and speak. Emotions ran high: many people were in tears, and the gathering continued through the night and into the early morning. We were overcome by an overwhelming sense of betrayal at the brutal gunning down of the peaceful fellow students in Ohio. We wanted to know how this could happen in America.

Classes resumed a few days later, but a somber atmosphere had descended. We all believed this was a turning point in the war. I talked to my dad on the phone. He revered America and had honorably served his country many years earlier. I could sense the disgust in his voice.

"It's time we end this war," he volunteered. "Men are dying needlessly, and they don't even understand what they are fighting for."

Middlebury was an exceptional educational experience, and my last years there seemed to move along far too quickly. Wonderful friendships I developed with Dave Sheldon and others have lasted a lifetime. This was a time of great music. We had a lot of house parties, which always featured live bands and singers. I had formed close friendships with a number of people in the class ahead of me, and not having them around after they graduated in spring 1972 was the singular point of disappointment during my final year.

My interest in political science continued to grow, and class preparation also remained voluminous. I had developed a rhythm in my study habits and kept my grades high enough to stay on the dean's list each semester. During my senior year, several interesting scholastic episodes framed the end of my college days. Poli-sci majors were not required to write a senior thesis, but we did have to submit proof of original research. When Salvador Allende became president of Chile in 1970, he was the first socialist in the western hemisphere to be elected to a country's highest post. I couldn't imagine a more interesting topic to research—but I faced a challenge of finding primary source material on voting and economic opinions in Chile.

I ended up driving to Princeton, to the Firestone Library at the university, where I located original works. I also sourced material at the University of Vermont's extensive library in Burlington. Allende was soon up for reelection, and my research indicated that he would likely not win. I accumulated an impressive amount of source material and began drafting a 100-page paper. My conclusion was that Allende would not be reelected because he lacked support among the middle class and from the younger middle ranks of the military.

I concluded my findings by predicting that Chile would undergo a peaceful transfer of power the next year. I based this somewhat on knowing the government in Chile had not been overthrown in nearly 50 years. I presented my paper to the department and received approval and praise. Fortunately, I received an A.

On September 11, 1973, Salvador Allende was assassinated in a military coup, which history has shown was supported by the CIA. My research was excellent—my conclusion, not so much.

As my college days were ending during my senior year, it seemed that following my dad into a legal career was the obvious choice. Charlie's father was also an attorney, and he had decided the same thing. In spring of 1973, he and I took the LSAT, the ETS Law School entrance exams. We had been told that the LSAT included a math section—not my strong suit. Neither of us had taken any math since high school.

To prepare, we drove to Princeton, where Uncle Tim was a math teacher at the Hun School. He spent a day with us, providing a refresher in basic math, including fractions, percentages, and simple algebra. We also went into New York City, to the NYU campus, and attended a two-day LSAT preview course. We had been warned that the LSAT, unlike the SAT, contained questions specifically designed to make the test taker stumble, including questions for which the correct answer was not provided. Maybe it was divine intervention, but we both did quite well on the test.

I applied to two law schools, the Rutgers Law School in Newark, NJ, and the School of Law at SMU (Southern Methodist University) in Dallas, TX. Charlie had decided he would go to SMU. I was accepted at both schools but decided that I would wait a year as I had also been offered a job at the First National Bank of Princeton. I was curious about exploring a career in banking and decided to postpone my law school admission for a year to see if I liked working at the bank.

After a wonderful graduation ceremony from Middlebury—but before I began my job at the bank—I had an opportunity to go with my family on a three-week trip to Africa that turned out to be an emotional cornerstone of my life.

This trip came about because in 1973 Dad became the president of the YMCA for the United States. This is a voluntary, full-time position, and despite the prestige, it was a demanding appointment, and he had to take a two-year leave of absence from the law practice to devote himself to the position. He also donated his YMCA compensation to the national Y organization. Much of his time was spent at the YMCA World Headquarters in Geneva, Switzerland, which meant he was away a lot. During my senior year at Middlebury, he was often at the YMCA's US headquarters in Chicago.

In the 1970s, the YMCA was one of the world's largest operators of refugee operations, and the world meetings were held in Kampala, Uganda. My father knew that bringing Tom and me along with him and Mom on this trip was an adventure of a lifetime across the African continent. In addition, he had arranged for me to be a designated voting delegate, representing the United States at the world YMCA meeting in Kampala.

The trip started in Cairo, the sprawling capital of Egypt and a major city through which the Nile River flows. We were greeted by local Y volunteers, all of whom were successful businessmen and women, and they hosted us in their homes, among family and friends, with unmatched hospitality. They also took us on private tours of the pyramids, and we enjoyed a special evening at the Sphinx, where on the desert floor and in darkness lit by millions of stars, we were presented with a historical narrative on Egypt, the pharaohs, and the building of the amazing structures sitting in silhouette before us.

Egypt and Israel were at war during the time we visited Cairo, providing a stark contrast to the joy and tourism of our trip. The city seemed to be living in a subdued chaos. Sandbags and gun emplacements were scattered throughout the city. The government issued a nighttime blackout, and no one could use their auto headlights. That meant cars were careening around busy streets, leading to a lot of accidents. This didn't make sense because streetlights were on everywhere, illuminating all major roads.

Our next stop was Addis Ababa, Ethiopia. The country's leader, Haile Selassie, had been emperor since 1930, and he ruled with an iron fist. In 1935, when Italy invaded Ethiopia and took over, he led the resistance with British military support and recaptured the country in 1941. Less than a year after our visit there, the country underwent a revolution that led to his ouster. The details of his death are murky, although many said he was executed at the order of the military government. In the years following Selassie's death, he became revered as the Black Messiah by the Rastafarian movement.

In Addis, we met Dad's friend Ed Makonnen, who was the country's Prime Minister. He was also a delegate to the world YMCA meetings, and I remember he had a kind and gentle personality. He invited us to his home for dinner with his family. It was a pleasant gathering, and we talked about various topics and enjoyed a home-cooked meal. Sadly, he was killed on the steps of the capitol during the revolution in 1974.

Tom and I learned the local food and dining customs in Ethiopia through trial and error. We had been told to stick to hotel dining, advice we quickly forgot as we started exploring the city. I was always a fan of spicy foods, but I was stunned by the heat and spiciness of the local Ethiopian food. Before long, we were experimenting with some of the street cuisine that was served in communal pots. I once reached into a communal pot and pulled out something best referred to as "mystery meat." I swallowed it down, and Tom did the same. Needless to say, he and I spent a night and the better part of the next day in agony and close to bathroom facilities.

Departing Ethiopia, we headed to Tanzania and the start of a moving introduction to the country's wildlife. We visited Olduvai Gorge, known as the "Cradle of Mankind," located on the eastern

Serengeti Plain in the northern part of the country. It is an immense ravine approximately thirty miles in length. Archeologists led by Mary and Louis Leakey unearthed some of the earliest human remains, including Homo habilis, which at the time of our trip was generally regarded as the first human.

After enjoying several days of safari and the raw beauty of the African plain, we spent the night at Ngorongoro Crater, located in a World Heritage site. Archeologists believe that prehumans lived on the crater floor more than three million years ago. It is the world's largest volcanic caldera and covers 100 square miles, with a floor 2,000 feet below the rim where we stayed at the lodge. The vistas in the clean mountain air were magnificent and unobstructed.

After dinner, Tom and I were escorted back to our cabin by a guard carrying an automatic weapon. He warned us in broken English about the lions that frequented the pathway.

The guard unlocked the heavy doors, and we noticed steel protection and bars on all the windows and doors. The guard said the steel provided a barrier against elephants who, in times of drought, attempt to break into the cabins because they can smell the water in the bathroom.

In the daytime the temperature had been close to 100 degrees, but it had dropped into the low 40s at night. We could see our breath as the guard lit a woodstove and departed, locking the door behind him. The next morning, the guard woke us up with hot tea at 4:00 a.m., before sunrise. He took us out of the cabin, and we could tell right away that the temperature had fallen further as we exited the cabin. We walked a distance to where we watched in silence as the sun rose above the rim of the volcano. As the early rays hit the enormous lake on the floor 2,000 feet below, it reflected hot pink. It was a striking and iridescent sight.

The guard smiled and shouted, "Flamingos!"

More than a million flamingos were standing in the shallow water and fanning their feathers to dry in the morning sun.

In the Tanzanian city of Dar es Salaam, we met Clem, a YMCA volunteer, and his family. Clem was a Pakistani who owned a printing firm. We had a wonderful time with them, and friendships developed rapidly.

At the time, Communist Chinese ships were docked in the harbor. The Chinese were training mercenaries to act as Rhodesian insurgent troops. Many businesses were being seized by the government, and they were paying pennies on the dollar. Years later I learned that Dad had transported a suitcase of money out of the country for Clem.

On Saba Saba Day, Tanzania's Independence Day, Clem took us on a multiple-hour drive to see Bagamoyo, among the oldest slave-trading posts in Africa. It was a forbidden place to visit for tourists and civilians.

As we arrived, children of all sizes and ages came to us and rubbed our hands. They had never seen a white person, and they had wonder and hesitancy in their eyes, something you rarely see anywhere in today's age of globalization. We toured this small village for an hour or two and returned on the one-lane, sand jeep trail. We were making good time when suddenly out of the jungle and from the thick curtain of trees and bushes emerged a band of a dozen or so Chinese and African fighters holding AK-47s pointed directly at us.

The rapidness of their appearance from the bush was terrifying and seemed to freeze time. Without missing a beat, Clem began speaking to them seamlessly in English, Swahili, and Chinese, all with a congenial smile on his face. He was the perfect diplomat at that moment. Fear in the instant made it impossible for me to think, and my head swarmed with chilling possibilities. They could kill us and kidnap us, and no one would know what happened to us. After a few tense moments, they lowered their guns and started to smile. They disappeared into the thick jungle as rapidly as they had appeared.

Once we got back to Dar es Salaam, for the main festivities of the Saba Saba Day, Tom and I were the only whites among the hundreds of thousands of Africans. We were right in front of the stage, swaying with the rest of the crowd, when Julius Nyerere, the president of Tanzania, came on the stage. He gave a passionate speech accompanied by fist bumps and a lot of pointing toward the crowd, which responded eagerly with songs, claps, and hollers. People were chanting, dancing, and crashing into one another as if in a trance. It was an amazing experience to be caught up with them like that.

We were coming to the end of our visit in Tanzania when we learned that a US Peace Corps plane en route to East Africa had been forced down by Uganda Air Force jets and made to land at the Entebbe airport. Our next stop was Nairobi, Kenya, before our final destination, in Uganda. After this incident, our State Department issued a travel warning, advising US citizens not to travel to Uganda. Understandably everyone in our delegation was concerned and confused about what we should do.

My father gathered everyone for a meeting to discuss the situation. Ugandan President Idi Amin had already contacted the delegation and assured us that all members would be safe, and he extended a warm welcome to us to enter Uganda.

The room was very tense, and as young as I was, I decided to speak up and express my views. I said that after having traveled so far to attend the world meetings, I was comfortable accepting the assurance offered by President Amin.

My father smiled and readily agreed. Ultimately, a vote was taken that led to unanimous support for us to continue our travels and go on to Kampala. We left Tanzania and flew to Nairobi, Kenya, where we spent several days on safari, including stops in Mombasa and safaris in the enormous national parks.

In 1973 African wildlife was much more abundant than it is today. We saw an exceptional array of animals in their natural environment, including lions, cheetahs (one with two cubs), leopards, giraffes, water buffalo, zebras, and an amazing variety of gazelles. Most of the time, our Land Rover was able to get within 20 to 30 feet of them.

As an example of the dramatic reduction of wildlife on the continent, there were approximately 1.4 million elephants in 1973 and less than 400,000 in 2020. The declines are largely at the hands of poachers who indiscriminately killed tens of thousands of elephants for their tusks, which were prized particularly by wealthy Asians. The elephants were brutally slaughtered, their tusks were removed with chain saws, and their carcasses were left to rot in the hot sun. The number of rhinoceroses also declined from 70,000 to only 27,000 today. They too were killed indiscriminately by poachers. Rhinos are prized in Asia for their horns, which some cultures believe have curative and sexual powers. The rare black rhinos, which we saw on safari in 1973, have fared even worse. Fewer than 5,500 are thought to be alive today, and none of them exist outside of parks and reserves. Unbelievably, only two known white rhinos are alive. They are kept in a reserve under 24-hour-a-day surveillance.

After our time in Kenya, we traveled to Kampala, Uganda, for the world YMCA meetings.

Idi Amin Dada Oumee was born in Kampala, Uganda, in 1924 His father abandoned him at a young age, and he lived with his mother until young adulthood. In 1946, he joined the King's African Rifles, a multibattalion British colonial regiment. By 1959, he had worked his way up to warrant officer, the highest rank possible at the time for a Black African in the British Army. This was an achievement and an honor, which made him a favorite of the British Army. A native descendent of the Kakwa and Lugbara tribes, he was noted for recruiting its members into the army.

When Uganda gained its freedom from British rule in 1962, Amin became a major in the Ugandan Army. Just three years later, in 1965, he was promoted to the commander of the Ugandan Army. Amin was an impressive man of 6'4 who had proven himself as a star of hard-hitting sports. He played rugby in the forward position and was known for plowing into his opponents on the field. Also, while he was rising in the Ugandan military, he was the country's heavyweight boxing champion from 1951 to 1960. All this combined to establish Amin's reputation as a man of intimidating strength and ruthlessness. In January 1971, after learning that Ugandan president Milton Obote planned to arrest him for misappropriation of army funds, Amin staged a coup. It was a gamble, but his time in the military had gained the trust or at minimum the intimidation of countless men, and he could rely on them to follow him now.

Amin first led troops loyal to him in taking over the Entebbe airport, and then they surrounded Obote's residence. Their next move was to seize control of the radio station and to begin broadcasting reports and accusations of Obote's corruption. This threw Uganda into a political chaos, with Amin and Obote claiming to be in control of the government.

Amin freed hundreds of prisoners and declared that he was forming a "caretaker government." A week later, he pronounced himself president and commander in chief of the armed forces, and Obote's supporters were purged from the military. Shortly after, he suspended provisions of the Uganda Constitution and created military tribunals with control over the civil courts.

As rumors spread about the torture of Amin's political opponents, 20,000 Ugandan citizens took refuge in Tanzania. It was chaos and anarchy. People did whatever they thought was necessary for them to survive. Self-reliance was the only reliable currency as loyalties became fickle and were easily bought.

The western media largely failed to cover these events, as they rarely do with stories about the African continent. Many years after the Ugandan coup, it was revealed that Amin had been behind the mass executions of rival Acholi and Langi ethnic groups. University professors, business leaders, journalists, judges, lawyers, and foreign nationals disappeared and were never seen again. Thousands of families lost loved ones to violence. Amnesty International estimates that Amin-sponsored genocide resulted in 500,000 deaths.

When our delegation arrived in Kampala, Amin had been Uganda's president for a little more than two years. I had read that some biblical scholars believe the Garden of Eden had been in Kampala. Early accounts describe its lush rolling hills with verdant trees and plants and its moist air suffused with hibiscus and lavender. That may have been so at one time, but it was something else entirely in 1973. The entrance to the InterContinental hotel, where we stayed adjacent to the convention center, was lined with sandbag-fortified machine-gun emplacements. Soldiers with automatic weapons were stationed on the roof. Tom and I entered our room, and the beds were unmade and looked slept in. We decided it might be best to sleep on top of the blankets.

A welcome reception was planned for the first night, and we walked over to the convention center with Mom and Dad. More than 500 delegates from more than 70 countries had gathered to attend the world YMCA meetings. There were approximately 80 members of the US delegation. At age 21, I was the youngest US delegate.

Our hosts had arranged long tables with an incredible display of fruits and cheeses, and they had live music playing—yet there was something incongruent about the atmosphere. The waiters were tense and glanced around the large entrance hall. None of them smiled or greeted us. It occurred to me several months later that they were terrified.

A hush fell on the hall as the music stopped, and President Idi Amin entered. He strode to the front of the room and made some brief remarks during his welcome speech. The music started up again, and he began to wander around the hall. Suddenly he was standing in front of me with a congenial smile. He was perfectly dressed in a dark suit, club tie, crisp white shirt, and black shoes polished to a mirror shine.

THE PRINCETON PACKET

Princetonian Meets Dada

Rip Mason, son of Mr. and Mrs. Ralph Mason of Princeton, greets Uganda President General Idi Amin Dada at a reception for the 430 delegates from 57 nations attending the Sixth YMCA World Alliance Conference held in Kampala from July 1? to 25. General Dada had ordered the retention of U.S. P?ce Corps members shortly before the arrival of the YMCA ??y. He greeted and treated the YMCA delegates warmly.

President Idi Amin Dada Kampala, Uganda. 1973

My hand disappeared in his enormous grip when he took mine to shake it. He asked me who I was and was delighted to learn that I was from America. His English was refined with a distinct British accent.

"Where are you in school?" Amin asked me.

I told him I had attended Middlebury College, and he nodded to indicate that he'd heard of the school and approved of it. He quickly turned to the present and asked what I thought of Uganda so far.

"Kampala is a beautiful city and so is the countryside," I said, looking at him to see if I had responded in the right way. He smiled as he moved along and said he hoped I would enjoy my visit to his country. At the time, I didn't yet know about his role in leading to the disappearance of tens of thousands of his citizens, the elimination of scores of professors and business leaders. If I had, perhaps I would have known to be more frightened of him.

Several evenings after the opening event, the delegates were invited to a reception and dinner at the presidential palace. The temperature was perfect that evening, in the mid-70s with low humidity. Everyone was looking forward to relaxing and enjoying the hospitality after a full day of meetings. The palace was an all-white sprawling building with large lawns and enormous flower beds. The local plantings in the garden were manicured and blooming.

In the back, a large swimming pool surrounded by a patio was the central feature, and the guests hovered around it. Exotically displayed fruits, foods, and beverages were arrayed on banquet tables. As Tom and I arrived with our father and mother, a live band was playing softly in the background.

We were all aware that President Amin had opened the door of his presidential home to 500 delegates in attendance from around the world. When he joined the reception, conversation again ceased, and voices silenced. He had everyone's attention as he warmly welcomed the delegates and then began wandering with his handlers in the crowd.

Several local journalists were there that evening, and one of them approached me with a reserved smile and a conspiratorial look. He looked my age, in his early 20s, and he glanced around to see if we were being observed before huddling close to me and whispering, "Do you still have slavery in America?"

I thought he was kidding, but the expectant look on his face told me he wasn't. He was visibly shaken and frightened as we spoke. I assured him that slavery had been abolished in the United States more than 100 years ago after the Civil War.

He was still uncertain and wary after my assurance, and he said that Ugandan school children were taught that slavery still persisted in the United States. I was shocked by this and didn't know what I could say beyond what I'd already said to assure him that what he'd been told was wrong.

He appeared very anxious throughout our whole exchange, and in the end, he excused himself, letting me know he would be in danger if someone overheard what we had discussed. I have never forgotten his fear and concern that physical harm could come to him. It also made me realize for the first time in my young life how fragile truth and safety are.

Later that evening, President Amin singled me out again and walked over to me. I was concerned that he'd seen me talking to the journalist, but I quickly composed myself. Once again, I felt my hand disappear in his enormous grip. I thanked him for the generous reception and entertainment. I complimented him on the building and grounds, and I also mentioned how beautiful the country was and told him about my readings about the Garden of Eden.

He smiled and thanked me and asked me if there was anything special I wanted to see while I was in Uganda.

Without a moment of hesitation, I responded, "I've heard that the Murchison Falls are an amazing site to see. I would love to visit there while I'm in Uganda."

Instantly his handlers began shifting among their ranks and appeared to be astonished at my brashness. The falls were controversial and had been off-limits to tourists for a number of years after some Canadian tourists had been killed there.

Amin took this moment to show who was in charge, and said with a bright smile, "You shall see the falls. Will tomorrow morning be convenient? My pilot will fly you there in my plane."

I was stunned he'd said yes and also thrilled about this unexpected adventure.

That evening I told my parents about this encounter and Amin's invitation. They were excited about the prospect of this adventure for Tom and me. In retrospect, the personal guarantee of safety implied by Amin surely calmed any reservations my dad had. Amin was aware that Dad was the head of the US delegation attending the meetings.

The next morning, Tom and I were picked up by the president's limousine and taken to the Entebbe airport, where the president's pilot welcomed us. He invited me to sit in the front right seat while Tom was seated behind me. We took off from the airport and within a few minutes, we were over the jungle and flew for an hour or so to the falls. There was a grass landing strip inclined up a hill.

The pilot approached and first passed a few feet over the landing area. We looked down and saw zebras, gazelles, and a few water buffalo scamper out of the way. He returned after the circle, and we landed on the rutted runway.

Exiting the small plane, we were met by the staff in a Land Rover. They drove us farther up the hill to an enormous and impressive Victorian building. This was the lodge. It was all white with a wraparound porch. Standing there, the staff pointed out the Nile in the gorge below. Soon, we learned that no one from outside the country had been at the lodge for many years, and Tom and I appreciated what a unique and unprecedented opportunity this was. They served us a wonderful lunch and while we ate, we admired the solitude and raw beauty before us.

That afternoon we traveled down the hills to the Nile and boarded a small boat. As we pulled away from the shore, the falls were to our left. Hippos and crocodiles were in the water everywhere. The falls were a picture of unbridled natural beauty. At the top, the Nile is forced through a 23-foot opening in the rocks and tumbles 141 feet below. The roar was deafening, while the visual was monumental and incredible.

Historians believe that Roman soldiers in search of the source of the Nile reached the falls in 61 AD. The first Europeans who definitively saw the falls were Samuel and Florence Baker in the mid1800s. They named them for Roderick Murchison, the president of the Geographic Society of London. In 1954, Ernest Hemingway crashed a plane near the falls. The site is shrouded in the shadows of history and tragedy.

We were astounded by the abundance of wildlife around the area. Incredibly large birds of varying colors were in the sky or perched on the tree branches. The air was filled with their tweeting and chatter. Water buffalo stuck close to the banks of the river while hippos repeatedly bumped our boat. I knew it would not be a good time to capsize in a river with 20-foot-long crocodiles swimming beside the boat or sleeping on the riverbanks.

While we were there, I was struck that just a few weeks earlier, we had been on the banks of the same river in awe of the pyramids and the Sphinx. It was all over much too soon. We returned to the lodge for refreshments, then said our goodbyes and headed back to the plane for a gripping takeoff on the bumpy runway. Approaching the end of the takeoff area and a steep falloff on the hill, we were finally airborne and returning to Entebbe.

That evening, President Amin saw Tom and me and came over to ask about our journey. I thanked him profusely. He smiled brightly as I described the animals, the falls, and the hospitality he had arranged for us. It was truly an experience of a lifetime.

The Africa trip was an awakening on many levels. It was my first direct encounter with potential physical harm. Also, it was my first encounter with someone whom history has shown was a brutal mass murderer, intent on genocide. At the same time, it was an introduction to emotional, raw beauty as well as to some kind and gentle people. Africa is a land of contradictions, as viewed from this perspective.

The Africa trip was a head-turning experience, and when we returned, my plan was to live at home with my parents and work at the bank. Mom and Dad's house was comfortable, but at age 22 and after four years on my own at college, I discovered quickly it was time to move on. It also didn't take long for me to figure out that banking held little interest for me. After a few months, I thanked the executives for the great opportunity they'd offered me and departed for Colorado just as the snow was starting to fall in the Rockies. During my Middlebury years, I'd skied up to 100 days a year at the college ski area, and now that call of the mountains was overpowering.

Tom was attending Colorado Mountain College at the time in Glenwood Springs—a short drive from Aspen. He lived in an old trailer. I spent several weeks with him, sleeping on a couch and skiing until my cash eventually ran out. That meant it was time to return to Princeton and focus on making some serious career decisions.

My friend Dave Sheldon and I started working on the old and, at the time, dilapidated farmhouse in Harbourton. This summer house was very small, less than 600 square feet, and it had been such an important place in my childhood. Nobody had lived there or even used it for many years. The windows were boarded up, and a tree branch had grown through the wall in one of the back corners of the house. We replaced part of the roof, drove the nesting squirrels out of the attic, and replaced broken windows. We made it our project and set to work every weekend, determined to make it "livable," at least in the bohemian sense of the word at that time.

The house continued to be a work in progress over the coming years, but at the time it was our getaway. Word got around about what we were doing, and my cousin Jeff and my high school friend Skitch were frequent weekend guests. Tom had transferred to the

Rochester Institute of Technology, and when he graduated, he moved in along with my friend Doug Grau with whom I had worked for five summers at Camp Highlander in North Carolina. I still can't believe all of us were able to stay in that house at the same time, but we had a great time and built memories that would last forever.

This "Endless Summer" was fun, but I also had to get serious and decided it was time to go back to school. I enrolled at the School of Law at SMU for fall 1975.

Chapter 3

Law School, South Pacific, and Passing the Bar

Charlie had already made it through a year at SMU law, and I had heard many of his stories about the workload and stress of that first experience. Even so, I was feeling academically qualified and I was probably a bit cocky, and I decided I could skip law school orientation and stay at the Harbourton farm with Dave, Tom, and Doug until the last moment. Two days before classes were beginning in Dallas, I loaded up my white Buick Skylark, put two pairs of skis on the roof, and hooked up a motorcycle trailer that carried my Honda. It looked more like I was heading to Club Med than off toward a serious academic pursuit.

Driving across the southern United States, I spent one night on the side of the road so I could get a few hours of sleep. The next day, I traveled across Arkansas and the eastern part of Texas, two states I had never before seen. This was late August, and as the sun rose higher in the sky, the air became torrid. The Skylark did not have air-conditioning. The temperature gauge eclipsed 100 degrees, and the clothes started coming off.

Many hours and hundreds of miles later, I arrived at SMU in Dallas. My shoulder-length hair was in a ponytail, and I was wearing red running shorts, no shirt, and white Adidas running shoes. Pulling up to the impressive and massive law library, I parked in front and bounded up the steps to the front door, which I threw open. Inside, the entire first-year law school class was immaculately attired in suits and ties for the dean's class-year opening cocktail reception.

One of the students, who saw the shock and embarrassment on my face, approached and said, "You look to be in the wrong place."

He offered his hand, and we both laughed. "I am Mark McQuality. Nice to meet you."

I had arrived in Dallas without a place to stay and somehow believed I could ease myself into the law school process. Mark and his roommate, John Phalen, offered me their couch while I looked for a place to live. The next day was the first day of classes, and Mark told me the assignments were already posted. He suggested I read the cases because they had been told during the orientation that the first day would be a sprint start. I had a fitful night on the couch after reading the cases.

The first class in the morning was property law with Professor Larson. The door outside the enormous lecture hall held a display of our seat assignments with our names and photos. My place happened to be adjacent to Mark's, and we sat down. I expected the class to begin with an overview of the school year and course of study, so I was stunned when Larson walked in, looked down at the seating diagram, and said, "I am Professor Larson. This is property law. Mr. Mason, tell us about the first case."

I did not have the case book, and Mark slid his over. I asked Professor Larson if I should stand, and he responded yes.

Law school proved to be very different from my college years. The process was designed to facilitate what appeared to be a mythical goal of teaching us "to think like a lawyer." This was a constant refrain. Gone was the verbose and flowery language of college, and it was replaced by terse and highly focused expressions of the facts of a case under review. There was a premium on the economy of words.

I was surprised that for the first year, we were grouped in sections of students and took all our courses together. Up to 150 students trundled from class to class, always sitting in assigned seats. Within weeks, admeasurement and a sense of internal competition were established in the section, and that was entirely the point. Class instruction followed the Socratic method, with the professor at the head of the lecture hall calling on a student to describe a case, a legal holding, and often the relevance to other cases previously reviewed.

The professor posed questions, frequently taking an opposing point of view, and as the student relented, switching again to an alternative viewpoint. Occasionally, these exchanges were humorous. They were always intense for the student of the day, who often stood for an hour under the barrage. The classwork was exceptional. I often spent 12 hours each day preparing and reviewing the next day's assigned materials.

Throughout the first semester there were no quizzes, papers, or tests, and as a result, we didn't know if we really understood the materials and direction. However, at the end we had a three-hour final exam for each course. I was stunned during my first exam in December 1975 when I saw several classmates drop their pencils during the test, get up, and depart. After an intense and unrelenting first few months, they were done and were off to pursue whatever life held next for them.

Criminal law is one of the first-year courses required in law school. My criminal law professor, Walter Steele, was a legend and a former prosecutor with an intimidating air. He wore cowboy boots and dark suits, and when he strode into class, everyone stopped talking as he sat at the lectern. With no introduction, and without even looking up, he called out the name of a student and the confrontation commenced. In measured tones, Professor Steele asked the student to describe the facts of the case and the court's holding.

Concise responses were always expected—yet any absence of complete mastery of these basic elements was met by Professor

Steele's glare and scrutiny. The verbosity of college exchanges obliviated with terse, fact-based precision. I recall more than one occasion when he sat silently while a less-than-confident student fumbled with the facts. Finally, when the student stopped, the professor mumbled, "Sometimes I feel like I am on the moon." Other times, he stood up, closed his folio, and walked out of the lecture hall, leaving everyone to reflect in silence.

Professor Steele's exhausting sessions made everyone come fully prepared for class. When my inquisition came, I managed to emerge intact with limited scarring. One of Professor Steele's most common approaches was to present the opposing position to the student's recitation—which was always a support of the court holding. The professor's decimation of the court's theory of the case prompted the student to concur that the court was incorrect. That's when the professor switched to an intellectually rigorous defense of the court's ruling. It was always instructive to realize that opposite points of view could be manipulated to fit the facts of the case.

At the end of the semester, the criminal law final exam was looming, and I was concerned about my mastery of the subject matter. But upon completing the test, I felt secure that I had presented a more than ample exam. When the grades were posted, the results were indeed acceptable but somewhat less than I expected.

In a moment of daring, I asked Professor Steele if I could meet with him to review my test. He invited me up to his office, which could have doubled as a set for a Law & Order episode. Sitting across from me behind an enormous desk, Professor Steele handed me my test booklet. I noticed the absence of any red marks or notations on the first three or four pages. Then I turned to a page with a red stamp that said "BULLSHIT." I looked up, curious to learn what this meant. He was smiling, and in a heavy Texas drawl, said, "Look, son, everyone starts with 100 on the test. I count the bullshit, and that is the grade. You did well, Mr. Mason. Now, get the hell out of my office!"

My friends and I eventually became accustomed to the pace and intentional stress of law school and sought release and a break whenever possible. We didn't seem to require much sleep at the time, and once we'd concluded our preparation for the next day's classes, we frequently met around midnight for beers at local bars. In those days, Dallas was a city of music, and even the smallest bars always had live music. Most of this was called country-western then, and it was a new sound to me. I grew to enjoy these late-night (early-morning) gatherings and to develop a taste for the music.

The summer of 1975 was my parents' 25th wedding anniversary. Dad served in the Pacific during World War II. He had always delighted us with his stories about the exotic islands in French Polynesia where he was stationed. Years after his death, these stories are a reminder of how fulfilling his life was.

As kids, like most American families, we used to gather in front of the TV every Sunday evening to watch the Magical World of Disney show. The creators at Disney managed to capture children's imagination. Years have passed, but our family reunions are still incomplete without mentioning those Disney Sunday nights and the nostalgia they bring.

Dad promised to take us to Disneyland someday, even if that seemed like a far-off dream. We knew Dad always kept his promises, so it was just a matter of time and opportunity. The trip to Disneyland finally arrived in June 1975 when we boarded the flight to Los Angeles.

Karen, Tom, and I were in our 20s—22, 20, and 24 years old, respectively—and we were long past dwelling in our childhood dreams Disneyland was an exception. With laughter and a whiff of nostalgia, we rode the teacups and the Dumbo ride together. The two rides were the ones we'd most wanted to take when we were little.

The next day we left Los Angeles and flew for more than nine hours across the Pacific to Papeete, the capital of French Polynesia, on the island of Tahiti. The volcanic mountains painted the horizons in muted grays. Lush vegetation was everywhere, and the air was permeated by the beautiful fragrances from millions of native flowers. The black sand beaches were decidedly different than those of the Jersey Shore, and I was mesmerized by the island's never-ending beauty.

The landing in Papeete was eventful. A car pulled up just when the airport staff was setting up the boarding stairs for the passengers. The pilot's voice rang out in the plane, advising the passengers to remain seated. No one inside the aircraft moved, heeding his caution. Suddenly, a man emerged from the car on the runway and ran up the stairs into the plane. He looked around the aircraft with eager anticipation. His eyes lit up when he spotted Dad.

In an instant, he rushed up to my father and caught him in a bone-crushing hug. They fell into an easy conversation and laughter immediately. The rest of the passengers and I looked on, smiling at the heartfelt reunion. Later, we learned that the man, who was now a wealthy government official, was the officers' club "house boy" in Bora-Bora during World War II. That evening he took us to his house for dinner with his family. We were sitting around an enormous round table for dinner, and my dad asked, "Is this the table from the officers' club?"

Our host paused, then smiled before replying, "Yes!"

He and my dad seemed to be remembering some inside joke and both burst into a fit of laughter. Over dinner, we learned more about Dad's time in Bora-Bora and his friendship with the local staff. I could tell from what my dad said that he'd been helpful to his house boy, who had made a life for himself and become a wealthy Polynesian landowner.

Several days later, we took a short flight from Tahiti to Bora-Bora. Once again, I was mesmerized by the natural beauty. A reef protected the island with waves breaking approximately a half mile offshore. Tom and I rode bicycles around the island, soaking in our surroundings. We spent the next few days snorkeling, gathering shells, and enjoying our cabana, set out over the water, with a plexiglass floor. At night, we drank beers and watched a fantastic variety of fish and stingrays swimming in the glow of underwater light.

Tom had received his scuba-diving certification just before our trip, and we asked about arranging scuba diving at the hotel. Apparently, there was only one person, Erwin Christian, who could authorize water activities in Bora-Bora. The hotel staff contacted Erwin for us, and the coveted nature of his authority turned our experience into an exclusive opportunity.

We met Erwin the day of our dive and traveled a short way off the shore in his small outboard. It was my first time scuba diving, despite my snorkeling experience. I was surprised at our anchorage as we were only 100 yards from the beach. Erwin helped us put on our tanks without briefing us about the process. None of us other than Tom had scuba certification. Without giving us any instruction, Erwin jumped in the water with a spear gun in hand and water splashing everywhere. Moments later, he broke out of the surface of the water and said, "Follow me."

Tom jumped in after Erwin and I joined him into the water after inserting my mouthpiece. The water was crystal clear and warm. We were immediately surrounded by fish of every imaginable size and color. Surprisingly, the volcanic coral reef disappeared steeply into darkness. As we swam out only a short distance from the shoreline, I discovered that the bottom fell off rapidly by more than 500 feet. We were down approximately 50 feet when Erwin started to spear some fish. His movements looked practiced. The gored fish spread blood throughout the water.

Attracted by the blood, one, then two, and then finally three blacktip sharks came toward us and started circling Erwin, who was holding the speared fish. Even as menacing as the sharks were, he refused to give up the fish and began parrying the sharks with the shaft of his speargun. Tom and I backed into the coral slope, searching for safety. Erwin was somehow able to get the sharks to leave, and he came up to join us, still carrying the fish. The whole thing had been insanity on his part, to be honest. Our adventure was nearly over, so we started ascending slowly toward our boat. On our way there, we saw a huge Napoleon fish about 10 feet long and shaped like a giant sunfish.

We emerged from the water reliving the excitement of the dive and the shark encounter. We enjoyed a cold beer in Erwin's boat, and I asked him to join us for cocktails back at the hotel, where he could meet Mom, Dad, and Karen. As the matter was settled, I asked Erwin how he enjoyed the exclusive water rights for the entire island.

Erwin smiled and said, "Rip, haven't you figured that out? My great-grandfather was Fletcher Christian, the leader of the mutiny on the Bounty in 1789."

The next morning, we departed on a sailboat for the neighboring islands of Huahine, Moorea, and Raiatea. Each one was a magnificent tropical paradise. We stayed aboard the boat or in cottages on the beaches.

Much of the sailing was in open water, with occasionally heavy seas. Karen was a good sport and rarely complained, but she was seasick and had to lie down on the deck with a cold towel on her head. She discovered that the location on the boat with the least movement was the center of the deck. Tom and I ran around the boat or climbed the rigging with a beer in hand. It was another wonderful and memorable family trip together.

At the midpoint of my second year of law school, with Charlie's graduation the next spring, and the realization that my legal career would be focused in New Jersey, I accepted admittance to attend Rutgers Law School in Newark and decided to transfer there, starting in January 1976.

I was reunited with my brother and Doug Grau when I returned to the residence at the Harbourton farm in mid-December. Tom had purchased a small woodstove that was in his bedroom on the first floor directly below my room. Unfortunately, no one had thought this through, and there was little wood harvested to build fires. We set to work gathering anything that was combustible: deadfall tree limbs, freshly cut trees (which do not burn without a year of seasoning), and, on more than one occasion, furniture. It was a primitive existence.

The half-mile gravel lane leading to the house froze solid in January, and none of us had four-wheel drive vehicles. We had to leave our cars on the road at the end of the drive. We carried everything, including a great number of cases of beer, the distance to the house. There was much laughter at our ineptitude. Dave showed up every weekend, and Jeff often joined us for TV sports and also to help scour for firewood.

In mid-January, classes at Rutgers began. The quality of the professors was at least on par with SMU, but the Rutgers faculty was decidedly more liberal, and several of them had argued cases before the United States Supreme Court on behalf of progressive causes. The school well deserved its moniker as the People's Electric Law School. My daily travels to Newark were interesting. I went to the Hopewell train station and boarded the Reading Railroad train. This was a two-car train, and the first one was a bar car. There were only two trains up to Newark every morning and two trains home. I soon discovered a group of about a dozen commuters—all executives who were immaculately dressed—boarded the train every morning before dawn at the Main Line near Philadelphia and sat together for the multiple-hour ride to Newark and on to New York. The engineer on my train, the first one in the morning, had a day job as a banker in Newark. He drove the train to the station and got off there along with the passengers and went to work at the bank. In the evenings, the same engineer-cum-banker boarded the train and drove the passengers home.

I typically spent my time on the train to Newark reviewing the case assignments for classes that morning. On the way home, I started to read the assignments for the next day.

One evening shortly after we departed the Newark station, the conductor, Junious, an enormous African American man, tapped me on the shoulder. "Mr. Tausig wants to speak with you."

Ralph Tausig was known to everyone as the unofficial mayor of the train. I followed Junious to the bar car where I found Ralph sitting with three other Wall Streeters, enjoying a martini. One of them stood up, offering me a seat, and introductions were made. Ralph addressed me, "I see you on the train every day with law books. Are you taking tax law?" I responded affirmatively. He paused and then asked me an interesting and complex tax question, encouraging me to share my views.

"That is a great question," I responded. "Give me a day, and I will be back to you."

He asked if I wanted a drink. "Of course," I said. (I could never afford one on the train.) I asked for a Budweiser, and in less than a moment, a perfectly cold beer was on the table. We swapped stories for another hour until we reached Hopewell, and I departed the train. The next afternoon Junious was again at my shoulder. "Mr. Tausig will see you." I walked back to the car, and a cold Budweiser was already waiting for me.

"I have some ideas about your question," I said to Ralph. I grabbed a napkin and with a pen began diagramming the tax issue. I had to flip the napkin over to draw two more potential approaches. I looked up and saw that Ralph was smiling.

"Rip, it took my tax team a week to come up with that analysis. I think you should have another beer."

The men at that table welcomed me to sit with them every day for the next year and a half, and I never paid for a beer. These Wall Street giants became my first clients. I learned so much from them, and I am forever grateful they gave me an opportunity.

In Spring 1977, as I neared graduation from Rutgers Law School in June, I interviewed with my dad's law partner, Gordon Griffin, about a job at the firm. Soon after, I was offered a job at Dad's law firm in Princeton. A rite of passage faced by all lawyers, once they graduate from an accredited law school, is the successful completion of the bar exam. The ability to translate four years of college and three years of law school into a career was entirely predicated on two days of testing.

The first day was another ETS exam known as the Multistate Bar Exam. The second day was essays. The testing was largely focused on what we'd learned in the first-year core courses. A cottage industry had sprung up to prepare potential lawyers for the test. It was known as a bar review course. Every student I knew at SMU and Rutgers participated in a six-week bar review course. Only about 40 percent of qualified test takers passed the New Jersey bar exam on their first attempt. Once again, the pressure was on.

I was living at the Harbourton farm with Tom and Doug, and early that spring, I told them I needed to focus completely on preparing for the test and asked if they would move out for two months. They knew this was the ultimate challenge to me becoming a lawyer and agreed to give me the time I needed, as did Dave and Jeff, who respected my need for privacy in preparation.

I was already running and working out daily to keep in shape. After Tom and Doug departed, I doubled my workout. I ran every morning and again at night, and I was lifting and doing crunches and hundreds of push-ups. By late July, as the first testing day arrived, I was in terrific shape mentally and physically.

All test takers were required to present a birth certificate and photo ID to validate their identities and to be fingerprinted at a NJ State Police or local police station. Each day those taking the test were fingerprinted upon entering the lobby leading to the exam room. This was repeated if we left the exam room, even if we got up to use the bathroom.

We would not get the results of the test until December. For five months, each applicant lived in a self-imposed purgatory.

At the end of day two, when I was finished with the exam, I had a joyous reunion with Tom, Doug, Dave, and Jeff. I knew this waiting time might be my last opportunity for a lengthy getaway for many years, and I had decided to ride my motorcycle across the country that summer. It was an amazing journey. On August 16—the day Elvis died—I arrived in Dallas to visit Mark and John and stay at their rental home on Turtle Creek.

I called Tom, knowing he was heading to Wyoming later in the month to go rock climbing at Grand Teton National Park. We agreed to meet at the Climbers' Ranch in Teton on my 26th birthday—August 21, 1977. The park was 1,250 miles from Dallas and included a lengthy desert crossing. The daytime temperatures were over 110 degrees. Parking my motorcycle at a gas station in the desert, I watched as the bike started to list to the side—ultimately falling as the footrest disappeared into the soft asphalt. I decided from then on to take it easy during the day and travel at night.

Tom's instructions to get to the Climbers' Ranch were a bit general—at best: "So as you get to Jackson Hole, there is a town square," he'd said. "Take the road exiting town at the northwest corner of the square. Go about 10 miles. There is a dirt road on the left. No sign or street name. Take that left turn. About five miles later, there is a very small sign on the left that says, 'Climbers' Ranch.'"

On the morning of my birthday, I still had several hundred miles to drive through the mountains of Wyoming. I found the town square and took what appeared to be the northwest road out of town. Many miles later, I turned onto the dirt road. Driving for a few minutes on the straight roadway, I noticed a cloud of dust at least a mile ahead. As the dust ball came closer, I could see an orange glow. It was Tom in his bright orange Volvo. We stopped in the dust of the road, hugged, and laughed.

Chapter 4

Legal Career, the Long Trail, and Marriage and Family

I was back in my home state when I learned in December that I had passed the New Jersey bar exam. I went with Mom and Dad to the War Memorial in Trenton, where I, along with other successful candidates, was sworn in by New Jersey Supreme Court chief justice Richard J. Hughes.

Dad had my announcement cards mailed to all the firm clients and our family, notifying them of my association with the firm. My starting salary of $12,000 a year seemed a princely sum. The firm declared that my time would be billed at $25 an hour. I could not imagine anyone paying $25 for my advice and counsel.

Many in the legal community of Princeton and beyond referred to my father as the "Dean of the Bar." With his white hair and nice suits, he cut an impressive figure as a highly experienced lawyer. Indeed, his calling was as a counselor to his clients, and they included nationally famous heads of industry, such as Ed Griffiths, who ran General Electric, and Bill Schreyer, the CEO of Merrill Lynch. Though my dad's specialty was estates and trusts, including related tax matters, he was often sought out by his clients about operational and personnel matters that arose in their companies.

My dad and I had always been close. When I graduated from law school and became an associate in his firm, he was my boss, but working together didn't change our relationship. My mom observed that in the past he had never talked about work at home, but now I was over at their house for dinner three or four nights a week, and he and I openly discussed the matters we were working on and frequently laughed about the antics of certain clients or peculiarities of members of the firm.

Dad had a quiet demeanor. He ran the firm based on consensus, but if an attorney was out of line or embarrassed the firm in court, he would step in forcefully. I noted early on that he was always accorded respect and great deference—but he never sought it. He was a natural leader with great instincts for talent, and he appreciated hard work and dedication. He loved the practice of law. His expertise in estate taxation was recognized nationally and led to appearances before congressional committees reviewing proposed tax law revisions.

When I started in December 1977, the firm had approximately 18 members. Several were specialized lawyers in areas of zoning, municipal law, family law, and complex litigation. As the new guy who was developing my practice, I worked on assignments with all of them. I found out quickly that the course of study in law school was predominantly theory based. Knowledge of long-held principles of contract law, property law, torts, and criminal law had little application in the realities of serving clients. I was starting all over again. Would this ever end?

The firm was often hired by towns such as Princeton, Hopewell, and Hightstown to represent them and to provide legal services that included acting as a prosecutor for the town. These were highly sought-after contracts that many firms tried to get. It fell to me to become the prosecutor in Princeton Borough, Princeton Township (a separate entity), and Hightstown. These were night courts. The Princeton Borough Court convened at 6:30 p.m. every Monday, while the Township Court met every Tuesday evening.

Following a full day at the office, where I was exposed to divorce and custody litigation, complex estate matters, personal injury cases, and other general legal issues, I headed over an hour early to prep the cases with the police officers. The dockets were jammed, and the court often went until midnight. Routinely I walked into work on Wednesday at 8:00 a.m. having already billed 35 hours. Sleep was a fantasy reserved for weekends. But trying literally hundreds of cases a year helped me build my confidence and an ability to think quickly on my feet.

Going up against talented lawyers, all of them far more experienced, in contested court cases was like a sporting event. Every week was the Super Bowl. And while my opponents had one case to try for the evening, I had dozens. I had limited time for preparation, but as my confidence grew, I became increasingly protective of the police officers, many of whom became friends. I developed a reputation as an aggressive advocate. The cops loved it, especially when I rode up to the courthouse riding my Norton Commando motorcycle, with my briefcase strapped to the back with a bungee cord.

Within a year, I was being offered contracts from other municipalities to act as their prosecutor. I secured an appointment in the neighboring town of West Windsor and made even more friendships within their police department.

Early on, my dad assigned an adoption case to me that led to the first of a number of appearances I made before Judge George Y. Schoch, the assignment judge for three counties in New Jersey. This designation represented an appointment as the chief among all superior court judges in these counties. The position came with exceptional authority and absolute control over which judges preside over any case (criminal or civil). He was a brilliant judge. He had been a great student and possessed an exceptional knowledge of the law. He was also mercurial and much feared among even the most skilled attorneys who appeared in his courtroom. He did not tolerate a tardy appearance or a lack of complete preparation and mastery of legal precedents touching any case.

The case assigned to me was not a typical adoption. The clients were a couple in their early 80s who had served as Christian missionaries. They were seeking to adopt a 17-year-old young man from South Korea who was an elite cellist studying at the world-renowned Juilliard School of music in New York. Adoptions were permitted up to age 18. The young man had received his draft notice from the South Korean government and was required to report for duty in early January. His only exception would be if he were no longer a Korean citizen. I prepared the consents and court filings and met the young man and the elderly couple the day of the adoption, which was the day before the court's recess for Christmas. The student was well over six feet in height and several inches taller than me. I was stunned to learn that the adoptions this day would be presided over personally by Judge Schoch in his expansive and ornate courtroom in the Trenton courthouse. The courtroom had a 40-foot ceiling. It was paneled in dark wood with amazing carvings, and there was an enormous bench that had the judge sitting at least six feet above the courtroom floor.

The room was crowded with new mothers and fathers, who tried to smile and to appear relaxed in the august surroundings with their young children, many of them crying babies. It was pandemonium. When Judge Schoch entered and ascended his bench, all conversations ceased. He had a big smile and greeted everyone with holiday and Christmas best wishes. This was not the fearsome judge I had been warned about. He said he'd kept this special ceremony for himself over the years and explained how much it meant to him. I was touched by his frankness and openness. The names of each child and parents were called, and the judge and his clerk led them into his chamber where he asked them to take a seat and relax, while he shared a story or two.

When my case was reached and we were escorted into chambers, I expected the judge to question why this couple would adopt this young man who would soon be beyond the age of adoption. Much to my surprise, Judge Schoch never mentioned the underlying reasons. He was congenial and congratulatory. The whole process was over in just a few minutes.

As we rose from our seats, the judge said to me, "Mr. Mason—can you remain here for a moment?"

As my clients left, his jovial smile disappeared. "Mr. Mason, if you ever appear in my courtroom again with your top shirt button unbuttoned and without your tie firmly in place, I will hold you in contempt of this court!"

In one motion, I buttoned my shirt, pulled up my tie, and apologized profusely, noting that I had not intended to show any disrespect to the court.

Judge Schoch gave a brief nod. As I turned to open the door, he called after me, "Tell your dad, Merry Christmas."

I was still living a bohemian lifestyle with my brother Tom and Doug Grau at my small farmhouse in Harbourton. My corporate life and emerging profile provided a stark contrast to the rustic life surrounded by our dogs and farm cats. Often on nights when I did not have court, the three of us headed out for Chinese food. This was one of our favorite delights. It was not expensive, and the food had a variety of flavors. We got to know many of the staff and owners of the restaurants, and when they learned I was a lawyer, they asked me questions about employment law and taxes. Ultimately, I was hired by several restaurant owners to represent them in the purchase or sale of their businesses.

In commercial transactions, the attorney utilizes his trust account to clear the transaction payments and distributions to banks, tax authorities, creditors, and the owners. As the date was coming up for my first restaurant closing, I called my client to give him my account information so he could wire funds for his purchase. In broken but understandable English, he said he was paying cash. The price was more than $750,000.

On the day of the closing, a van pulled up to our office in Princeton. Several men and my client came into the office carrying large brown shopping bags. Other lawyers looked out of their offices to see what was going on. I took them up our elevator to the second-floor conference room. The seller and his attorney arrived. All the conversation was in Chinese. A few moments later, additional men in business suits arrived and opened the bags that were full of loose cash, in a variety of bills, including ones, fives, and tens. The men took nearly five hours to verify the amounts and arrange the bills in neat stacks by denomination.

The entire 12-foot table was covered in money, and on many levels it was an instructive moment to see the careful attention and reconfirmation paid to the purchase proceeds, cash allocations to creditors, and finally the net distribution to the seller. It left me with a visual reference for the seemingly invisible aspects of money transfers and closings that would stay with me throughout my corporate career.

As part of the firm's representation of Montgomery Township, I appeared on their behalf to prosecute criminal cases. The New Jersey Neuro-Psychiatric Institute, located within the township, housed indigent mentally and physically disabled patients. The staff was generally compassionate and provided exceptional care, but several horrendous incidents occurred, and patients were injured or beaten. In one particularly disturbing case, a male nurse was arrested and charged with a felony for breaking the jaw and several ribs, as well as causing various internal injuries, of one resident.

The injured patient could not speak, and the county determined that they could not successfully prosecute the case with no witnesses to the crime. I prepared for the case with the police, and as the trial day arrived, I knew I was becoming agitated and had developed a personal interest in the outcome—something always best to avoid. The defendant was cocky and defiant, and the trial was a complete frustration. The judge repeatedly cautioned me to keep my voice down.

"You are a really tough guy, aren't you?" I said at one point. "Beating up a defenseless man confined to a bed." The court called a recess. As I walked by the defense table, I leaned over and whispered in the defendant's ear, "Hey, tough guy. I am going to meet you outside when the court is over and kick your ass."

The defendant was found not guilty and released. The cops knew what was going to happen and grabbed me as I was heading to the door. With smiles on their faces, they put me in a squad car and drove me to a bar for beers.

In early 1979, the Mercer County Bar Association was assembling a list of practice specialties, and I was asked what mine was. I asked how many could I choose from, and there were quite a few. I asked if any of them had no attorney listed, and I was told, "entertainment law." I immediately responded, "That is my specialty!"

In early June, I received a call from a plumber from Trenton who said he and several friends appeared in Rocky II, the sequel to Rocky, the highest-grossing film of 1976. He had been given my name as an entertainment law attorney by the bar association. The plumber and his friends were a cappella street singers, and Sylvester Stallone's brother, Frank, had asked them to sing a song with him for the movie because his band was unavailable. They also provided the music and the arrangement for the song, "Two Kinds of Love," and it was included on the soundtrack album. The credits were listed as "words and music by Frank Stallone." I asked if they had been paid. They had not.

I asked if they had signed a release. They answered yes, but the release recited a payment they never received.

Rocky was nominated for 10 Academy Awards and won three, including best picture. The film received critical acclaim and captivated audiences with the story of an underdog who unexpectedly lands an opportunity to box the heavily favored, world-title holder. Rocky was a modern David vs. Goliath tale. Rocky II was the most anticipated film of 1979, and it had just opened in 805 theaters across the United States. That evening I saw the movie—again, my clients were not acknowledged in the film credits. Frank Stallone was solely credited for the lyrics and music of that song. I took the case on a one-third contingency of recovery.

I had a sleepless night evaluating my clients' lack of credits for both the album and movie and considered my strategic and tactical approaches. In its first week, Rocky 2 had grossed $11 million—an exceptional amount at the time. Audiences were flocking to theaters to relive the emotion of the original film.

Early the next morning, while running on the dark country roads near the farm, I decided to focus on restraining the sale of the soundtrack album. I knew the same legal theories would apply to the movie as the album, but I believed a federal judge would be less likely to pull a blockbuster film from theaters than to stop the sales of a record album. If I succeeded in stopping the album, I could raise the stakes and go after the film, which was being distributed by United Artists.

I was well aware of how audacious an undertaking this was. I was 27 years old and had been practicing law for only 18 months. Considering the film's notoriety, not to mention the enormous expense of its production, I expected United Artists to wage an all-out, high-profile defense. I admit I couldn't help but see the obvious parallels between me, the underdog new lawyer, and the Rocky character in the first film going up against a formidable and sophisticated opponent with unlimited resources. Another David vs. Goliath story—and this time I was cast as David.

I started preparing affidavits and drafted pleadings to halt the album's sale in the United States. As the pleadings came together, I sought a temporary restraining order (TRO) to stop the album's sale. The courts will only grant this type of extraordinary relief upon a clear showing of irreparable injury. I focused on a little-utilized provision of the Lanham Act, a federal statute, also known as the Trademark Act of 1946, that governs trademarks and unfair competition and requires all goods shipped between the states to contain complete and accurate labeling. The album and its cover were being sold across the United States without credit to my clients for the song they wrote, and my premise was that the labeling was misleading and incomplete. This view of the Lanham Act had been used extensively in the regulation of the pharmaceutical industry. My brief stated that the record label and jacket were misleading in their failure to accurately attribute the composition of that song to my clients.

A final prerequisite to filing for a TRO is to notify your adversary in advance to give them an opportunity to appear before the court.

I called United Artists, the film's distributor, at their New York offices and got through to the general counsel's office. I told one of their attorneys I was heading down to the Federal courthouse in Trenton, and they could appear to contest or respond to my TRO application. I then called Judge Clarkson Fisher's chambers to let them know I was coming and the nature of my TRO. The clerk met me at the door, and walked me into the judge's private chambers.

As the door was closing, the clerk raised his arms in the classic Rocky pose, and I heard him singing the film's theme song, "Gonna Fly Now," which had been nominated in 1977 for an Academy Award, for best original song, and had been #1 on the Billboard charts. After 15 or 20 minutes, the door opened. "The judge will see you now."

Judge Fisher was from a movie script. A big imposing man, with a football on the credenza. He glanced at the affidavits and my pleadings, noting that my use of the Lanham Act was clever. I knew this was a seriously brash move. But I felt confident in my legal theory.

The judge asked if I had called United Artists and offered them an opportunity to appear. I told him I had. He asked me what the response had been.

"Your honor, I would rather not say," I replied.

He asked me to look at him and tell him exactly what they said. I told him that their response was two words, "Fuck you."

The judge chuckled and said, "Fuck them. I am granting the TRO. Now go out, call them, and tell them to remove the *Rocky II* album from all record shops in the United States by tonight." When I left the courthouse, I called the Trenton newspaper and the New York Times. Each ran the story in their next editions.

Now that I had secured the court order temporarily halting the sale of the Rocky II soundtrack album, I started to prepare pleadings to stop the album sales permanently. A part of the filings was a TRO to shut down the movie based on the same legal principles. Two weeks later, Judge H. Curtis Meanor, at the federal courthouse in Newark, heard my motion to stop the album sales permanently and the new TRO to stop the showing of the movie. On the day of the hearing, the media was gathered on the courthouse steps. My clients and I were surrounded as we entered the imposing and grand courthouse.

Bill Brennan, a former New Jersey assistant attorney general, was there with four other lawyers representing United Artists. Bill's father was U.S. Supreme Court Justice William Brennan. United Artists was taking this seriously now, and they were in a panic that this kid from New Jersey was kicking their asses.

I played a clip from the movie where my clients appeared, along with the credits that did not include them but gave all credit to Frank Stallone. Judge Meanor listened to the evidence and called Brennan and me to the bench. He suggested to Brennan that he speak with me in the hallway because he was inclined to grant the permanent injunction and issue a new TRO shutting down the #1 movie in America.

Bill Brennan and I stepped outside, and he greeted me with a big smile and offered me his hand. He noted the unique theory of my case. He said he had appeared before Judge Meanor a number of times, and he understood the message. Bill and the United Artists attorneys with him were impeccably dressed in Italian suits and ties, which was a sharp contrast to my clients who wore work shirts and jeans. I was wearing my new suit from Sears for the occasion. And in a nod to Judge Schoch, I had taken care to fasten my top button and had properly cinched up my tie.

Bill quickly made a financial proposal to settle the litigation. I conferred briefly with my clients right there and gave Bill a nod of acceptance. The release documents my clients signed at the time of the *Rocky II* filming provided for payments of $180. The settlement amount was significantly greater.

Over the years, I ran into Bill Brennan at local charitable events. We always relived those tense moments in the courtroom, yet still parted with a chuckle and a smile. This case was an important step as I was starting out in my legal and commercial career.

I appeared before Judge Schoch again several years after the adoption case. Even after I had served for a number of years as a local prosecutor, the New Jersey practice rules permitted me to take on superior court cases (for felony charges) as a defense attorney. A variety of defendants in felony criminal proceedings were aware of my reputation from my prosecutorial assignments and requested that I represent them. Many of them had been charged with drug offenses—sometimes involving large quantities of drugs. In criminal defense representation, once an attorney begins representing a defendant, they are required to serve in that role until the defendant is either convicted or acquitted. The court won't let you resign from a case even if you aren't paid. For that reason, all representation for criminal charges requires complete payment in advance, including for any motions or other services. As a result, the money was great and all paid up front.

This was the early 1980s, and the New Jersey courts were overwhelmed with caseloads. To address this, the New Jersey legislature had adopted a diversion system known as pretrial intervention (PTI), which became known to prosecutors and defense lawyers as the "one free crime bill," because first-time offenders could apply to the county prosecutor for diversion out of the criminal justice system. The prosecutor had discretion to admit or deny a PTI application. If accepted, the defendant's arrest records could be expunged unless they were arrested again in the next several years.

I was retained by a first-time drug offender, and after collecting my fees, I drafted an application for him to receive PTI. I was friendly with the county prosecutors and was surprised several weeks later to get a letter denying a PTI diversion, without any detail for the rejection. I called their office and still did not get any reasons.

I took the rather unusual step of filing a motion to review the prosecutor's refusal. This was uncharted waters, and my legal argument was that their discretion was not absolute, though the PTI legislation gave the prosecutor wide latitude. My search of the bill's legislative history revealed commentary by state representatives that a prosecutor's discretion could not be taken in an arbitrary manner. There was no definitive case law yet deciding this issue. Chances of success were slim.

The week before, the superior court clerk let me know my motion would be heard by the assignment judge—Judge Schoch.

Motion days were always stressful, and I hadn't slept much for a week because I had been up late reconfirming my research and the legislative records. On Motion days all attorneys sit on the courtroom benches like schoolchildren, without the clients. Every top trial lawyer was there, giving me no place to hide from the assembled talent. This was a gathering of the best of the best.

As Judge Schoch entered, the tension was massive. Several motions were called before me. One attorney approached the bar to state his legal arguments, and Judge Schoch glared down at him, and with a raised voice said, "Did you write this?" as he held up the pleadings. The lawyer responded yes, and the judge ripped the pleadings in half and threw them toward the dumbstruck attorney. "How dare you come into my courtroom with such shabby research," Judge Schoch said. "I've a mind to hold you in contempt right now."

All the oxygen in the room depleted. Grown men and women at the height of their careers looked terrified. Of course, the next case called was mine.

I approached the bar and started to speak and the judge interrupted me. He then turned to the prosecutor and asked, "Why do you think you have the right to be arbitrary in accepting or denying a PTI application?"

The prosecutor meekly replied that the legislation empowered the prosecutorial discretion, but the judge responded, "That's not absolute." He added, "Mr. Mason, this is likely a case of first impression—the court has not seen another case on this narrow reading of this legislation. Good work digging into the legislative history. I'm granting your motion. Your client is now eligible for PTI on the order of the court." Professor Steele, my SMU criminal law instructor, would be smiling—and likely amused.

I closed my briefcase and looked around the courtroom as I got ready to depart. I received a number of smiles and thumbs-up from several of the prestigious and experienced litigators sitting there. In the coming years, several of them would reach out to me when they needed to refer a matter to someone else.

As my practice grew throughout the early 1980s, I developed an interest in negotiating and structuring commercial transactions. The lessons I had learned as a prosecutor about being prepared and thinking quickly on my feet were again helpful in these endeavors, when I was often working with highly experienced and much older attorneys and their clients. This specialty put me in contact with other influential and complementary service providers, including accountants, bankers, and insurance agents. Many of them were contemporaries, and not only did we enjoy one another's company, we frequently referred clients to one another.

By 1983 my book of business made me the second-highest money earner in the law firm. My dad was the first. I was 34 years old. Many of the other attorneys in the firm were in their 40s and 50s. I was made a partner that year, and my mom and dad put on a nice reception. All the attorneys and their spouses attended, along with several lead clients.

Dad enjoyed and encouraged my success and introduced me to several of his estate planning clients who were captains of industry. These corporate chieftains had me join them in boardrooms, and I became a trusted adviser and confidant.

In 1985, I was admitted to the New York Bar. Many of my new clients were running corporations in New York, and it was an important addition for me to be able to practice there, particularly as nearly all major transactional financing, including bond issuances, came from New York–based banks. Private equity was becoming an important alternative to a public stock listing, and in several years, it would become a bridge between my law practice and my later career as a manager of large corporations.

In 1986, Dad let me know his friend and business associate Herb Hobler, the owner of radio station WHWH, wanted to step down and sell the station. Herb was one of Dad's clients for many years, and in the mid-1960s, he secured a license from the FCC to start a new radio station in central New Jersey. He was a Princeton grad and had spent his career as a broadcaster working for CBS and other major media in New York.

I recall being at the Hopewell farm with Mom and Dad in the early 1960s and listening for the new station when it signed on to the air for the first time. It was memorable. Dad was an investor and was the station's attorney, and he served on the board of directors. At the time, the central New Jersey market was served by stations broadcasting out of New York and Philadelphia, which meant there was no coverage of local news, weather, and sports. The station, which became WHWH (for Herb W Hobler), was an instant success and became the voice of Princeton sports—in particular basketball, when Bill Bradley played for the university and took the team to the Final Four in the NCAA tournament.

When I became a lawyer, Herb called me from time to time with assignments for the station. In the mid-1980s, radio stations were prized by advertisers and were selling at a premium. My corporate and transaction practice was growing rapidly. When Dad told me that Herb wanted to sell the station, I immediately thought of Lou Mercatanti, a client and a close friend, who, like me, was in his mid-30s. Lou owned several car dealerships and was interested in diversifying his holdings.

I arranged a meeting for Lou with Herb, and they hit it off right away. Over the next few days, we rapidly worked out pricing and major deal points. I represented Herb, and I arranged for another local corporate attorney to represent Lou. Another close friend, Beck Miller, was the head of credit at Barclays Bank, an old-school London institution making inroads in the US market. I was also their attorney. I set up a dinner with Beck and Lou, and in a few weeks, I arranged the financing of the acquisition for Lou.

Changes in tax law had been approved by Congress, and Herb could save significantly if the deal closed by the end of the year. My contract contained a penalty (equal to the tax difference), increasing the amount paid to Herb if the deal did not close by December 31. A lot had to be handled to meet that deadline, including FCC investigations and approval for the transfer. Barclays also required extensive but normal diligence to fund the purchase. November and December were a race against the clock. Lou and I often met with bankers, accountants, and other lawyers until midnight or later. We worked through the Thanksgiving holiday, and the Christmas season was a blur. I often returned home early in the morning, took a quick shower, and put on a clean shirt and tie before heading back to the office or running for the train to New York.

A few days after Christmas, we secured the FCC approvals and the bank financing commitment. This left only a few days for loan documentation (which can run 100 pages or longer) and closing preparation. Finally, on December 31, I met in New York with Lou, Herb, my dad, Beck, and a host of bankers, lawyers, and accountants, and we closed the deal just before midnight.

I discovered in later years that all significant deals go through this same level of stress. The WHWH sale was similar to conducting an orchestra and came together at the right moment. Each player was in tune with the rest of the assembled group, all playing as one.

With so much time committed to my law practice, I had little time for vacations. My brother Tom and my great college friend Dave Sheldon enjoyed hiking and being outdoors. When Tom was only 15 years old, he became the youngest person at the time to climb Mount McKinley in Alaska, at over 20,000 feet, the highest peak in North America. Tom was a graduate of the National Outdoor Leadership School in Wyoming. He was an accomplished hiker, rock climber, and outdoor leader. As Tom and the team ascended McKinley, one of the other climbers fell to his death in a tragic accident. The expedition never reached the summit as they worked to retrieve and return the fallen team member.

Tom, Dave, and I loved the Green Mountains in Vermont and decided to hike the Long Trail, a 272-mile stretch of wilderness that starts in North Adams, Massachusetts, at the southern Vermont border, and ends at the Vermont/Canadian border in an area known as the Northeast Kingdom. This trek, which is 50 miles farther than the distance from New York to Washington, DC, and twice the mileage from Los Angeles and San Diego, is the oldest hiking trail in America. It runs along the peaks of the massive Green Mountains, which extend the entire length of Vermont, and it included tens of thousands of feet of exhausting climbs.

We started this journey in 1981, taking our precious few vacation days and packing up for a week of extreme hiking and walking the trail. Each year we started at the spot where we'd ended the previous year. In 1985 we completed the 272-mile journey, and we would forever be known as "End to Enders."

The hiking was physically and mentally demanding. Carrying large packs and provisions for a week, we ascended hundreds of climbs, many with extreme and seemingly never-ending vertical sections. We loved the challenge and the isolation. Tom was an exceptional trail chef. We ate well and enjoyed the camaraderie—great physical challenges and abundant laughter.

In 1985, we were entering the final sections of the Long Trail in the remote northern region of Vermont known as the Northeast Kingdom. Departing north of Stowe, we ascended Belvidere Mountain—a vertical climb of more than 2,000 feet. We were completely alone on the trail, not seeing anyone until a solitary encounter on the last day, which provided humorous relief. The trail was increasingly wild the farther north we journeyed.

By day five, we were back in hiking shape after repeated steep climbs and descents. The day broke clear, but it was surprisingly warm and humid as we departed the shelter at Tillotson Camp. Open-faced Adirondack shelters are placed at various intervals the entire trail length; many of them were built in the 1930s and 1940s. They were a primitive but welcome relief every evening as we dragged into camp at the end of the day. The shelter placements meant that hikers did not have to carry tents, cutting down on weight for the Long Trail sections.

At noon, as we descended to Hazen's Notch, the air was dense with humidity. Temperatures rose to the mid-80s. Our last water for the remaining 12 miles of the day was taken from a stream. We were parched and filled up all our water bottles. Carrying our heavy packs, we started the ascent of Bruce Peak, a 1,000-foot climb—roughly equal to climbing the World Trade Center. Halfway up the climb, we began to hear thunder rumbling in the distance and saw clouds rolling in. The wind was picking up ferociously. We were drenched with sweat and exertion and could feel the temperature starting to plummet.

A few minutes later, about midpoint in the ascent, the rain started and within moments, the trail ahead was barely visible through a blinding and unrelenting downpour. We were all experienced hikers, and we knew that in the absence of shelter, our only choice was to push ahead. The temperature was dropping rapidly, and if we took even a brief respite at the top of the climb, it could cause rapid body temperature loss and hypothermia. Tom, Dave, and I had hiked together for years, and I knew they were making the same calculations without us having to discuss it. We each hiked daily at our own pace.

Typically, Tom was last as his pack weighted far more because he was carrying his photography equipment, including extra long-range lenses and camera bodies.

In less than 30 minutes, the temperature had dropped by 40 degrees. The winds were howling through the trees, and several limbs were already down. The footing on these climbs was always difficult, but now it had become slick and treacherous, making the descents perilous. Once we summited the peak, we had to make it down a trail that rapidly dropped off vertically for 700 feet. The wind and rain were still unrelenting, but we still made it past that point. We were exhausted but unable to stop and catch a breath as we reached the next pass and the trail ascended straight up another 600 feet to Domeys Dome. Tom, Dave, and I had not seen one another for more than two hours, as we each walked carefully to avoid mishaps. If one of us had to stop in these conditions because of a twisted ankle or serious fall, it could lead to hypothermia in minutes and loss of consciousness.

Descending at last to the road before the shelter at Jay Camp, our final destination of the day, I dropped my pack and pulled out a warmer shirt to wait for Tom and Dave. If there had been an accident, I would walk back on the trail to carry them out.

Several minutes later, Dave walked out, followed by Tom 10 minutes after. We were too exhausted to discuss what we'd been through the last couple of hours. Instead, we headed farther north on the now flat trail (thank goodness!) to Jay Camp. The shelter was an enclosed cabin with a woodstove and firewood inside. In moments, we had the fire roaring, and our dripping-wet clothes were hanging along the warming cabin walls.

We were finally able to congratulate each other for successfully crossing the path through the storm without incident. We knew our deep knowledge of one another and experience had contributed to a safe outcome.

The next day we faced our final climb, the ascent of Jay Peak, that would take us into Canada. The day emerged fresh and cold, and the incredible rain had washed away the humidity. We struck out early, knowing we were about to have 272 miles of the challenge behind us. As we were making the ascent, an enormous moose appeared out of the thick vegetation and crossed the trail merely 10 feet in front of me. As he crashed through the trees and shrubs, he did not even glance in my direction. He reminded me of the camels Tom and I rode near the pyramids in Egypt. This was his domain.

A short while later, as we were closing in on midmorning, a man appeared on the trail, heading the opposite direction with a dog. He was barefoot and completely naked, with not a stitch of clothing. As we passed each other, I said, "I like your outfit." Tom and Dave burst into laughter.

We reached a small clearing on the mountain, and that ended our 272 miles of hiking. There was a 24-inch monument on that spot. On one side, it says the United States of America, and on the reverse, Canada.

This wasn't the last of our hikes on the Long Trail. We returned to this area in Vermont for several summers and revisited our favorite sections as a kind of "Greatest Hits." In July 1989, Tom, Dave, and I went to Vermont to hike a beautiful section of the trail that starts with a very vertical climb up Mount Abraham, one of Vermont's highest peaks.

The top of the mountain is above the tree line with unobstructed views west across the Adirondacks in upper New York state and to the east, the White Mountains of New Hampshire. Our destination that evening was Glen Ellen Lodge, a favorite shelter nestled on the eastern slope of Mt. Ellen. It was a hot July day as we ascended Mt. Abe, with the heat peaking as we traversed, heading north to Mt. Ellen. Along the trail, I could feel that the heat and exertion had caused my fingers to swell, restricting the ring I was wearing that had once been Pappy's.

When Pappy died unexpectedly in 1971, my grandmother asked if I wanted to have any of his possessions as a remembrance. I responded that I would love to have one item—his wedding ring. For the next 17 years, my mom kept the ring for me in her bank deposit box. In 1988, Mom gave me the ring, and I tried it on for the first time. Pappy had large hands, and the ring was too big. I took it to a jeweler in Princeton, who reduced the size by cutting out a small piece of the ring and rejoining the ends to accommodate my ring size.

With my fingers swollen on the hike, I glanced down and saw that the ring had separated where the jeweler had made the cut, leaving a gap of 1/8 inch or more. But the ring remained snug on my swollen finger.

We reached Glen Ellen Lodge several hours later. We hadn't been there since 1982, seven summers earlier. The view east to the White Mountains was stunning as we sat in the sun, totally exhausted. A small but roaring mountain stream next to the shelter afforded us delicious ice-cold mountain water. Before long, all three of us were in the stream enjoying the coolness.

I glanced down and was stunned to discover that the ring was gone. My hand and fingers had contracted in the cold mountain water, and the ring had fallen off. It was an impossible situation. The water was frothy and bubbling as it hurtled down the mountain. There was no way to see the bottom. Dejectedly, I left the water. Tom and Dave found me in front of the shelter, and I told them what had happened. We were all quiet. They knew I had been wearing Pappy's ring, and the joy of exertion and success that day was replaced with sadness. After a few minutes, I got up and headed back to the stream. Tom and Dave asked what I was doing, and I said I was going to try to dam up or divert the water so I could search for the ring. They jumped up immediately and headed to the stream with me. I entered the water and reached down into the sand and rocks to scoop up a large handful of the sediment to throw to the shoreline. I glanced down at my exposed hands and saw the ring was sitting in the middle of my palm. I could not believe this and was holding back tears. I got out of the water and showed the ring to Tom and Dave.

We knew we had just experienced a mystical moment. Pappy was there with us, guiding me as he did when I was a young boy.

I think there is some truth to John Updike's quote, "We are most alive when we are in love." I have felt the truth of his words not once but twice, and both times in all its softness and brittleness.

For me, relationships have never been linear equations that can be solved with a fixed and tested formula. Trial and error are the beauty of a human bond because they give us the chance to be better at every turn. Making mistakes is only human, and it is understandable that when you or your partner makes one, it is easy to let go. Most important, trial and error serve as the cornerstone of our interactions with others.

I met Ellen in 1987, and we bonded over our common interests. We married in July 1988. We were supposed to marry in a well-planned ceremony, but my father was my best man, and the night before the wedding, he was admitted to Princeton Hospital. We were married in the chapel there.

Ellen had two sons, Chris, who was six years old, and Stevie, who was four years old, from previous relationships. After our marriage, we all moved into my tiny farmhouse in Harbourton. The boys loved playing outdoors and had unending energy and stamina that I could tell had the makings of great sportsmen. I signed up Chris to play hockey and to learn to skate in a local league. Any experienced eye would take one look at him and know that he was a natural; he had terrific balance and natural skating ability. I signed up as the coach of his team.

Coaching a group of young kids just beginning to learn the ropes of the game was a whirlwind affair. Imagine fifteen little guys struggling to balance themselves on their skates and falling constantly while their parents cheered them on anyway. It was chaotic and silly, but just the beginning. Clumsy beginnings do not always lead to clumsy results.

By the end of the season, many of them had made leaps and bounds in their progression and were showing an upward arc in their talents, especially Chris. He loved the rink, his teammates, and our early-morning trips there together. A few years went by, and we had young Stevie in the game at age five, and I was the coach of two teams. Chris's progress in the sport was astounding. His natural talent made him an asset at a young age. He was selected for the travel team that was known for drawing the best players in each age group from several hundred players. It was an impressive feat for such a young kid. I agreed to coach the travel team with my friends Don Mikalasi and Doug Hoffman. I was responsible for three teams, so the pressure was on.

In late 1986, Dad started losing weight. He was always very active, but his energy levels had started to decline. His doctor, Sandy Carney (nephew of Art Carney of *The Honeymooners*), ran extensive tests, and his initial concerns were focused on cancer. Ultimately, Dad was diagnosed with myelofibrosis, an exotic and poorly understood disease that attacks the production of red blood cells in the bone marrow. The disease has similarities to leukemia.

This was not easy for me to accept, so I took Dad to the Memorial Sloan Kettering Cancer Center in New York City to confirm the diagnosis. Dr. Carney gave me Dad's X-rays and test results but also a word of caution. He didn't think they would have ever seen this disorder before, and he said it was best that I not let the X-rays out of my possession.

Shortly after we arrived at Sloan, the head of pathology came up to the exam room. Dr. Carney's words rang true because the doctor confirmed that he had not seen the disease previously. It took them some time to wrap their minds around the situation, but eventually, they confirmed Dr. Carney's diagnosis. My spirits were crushed when they said there was no cure for myelofibrosis; there still isn't today. At that time, there was only one doctor who was a specialist in the disease, and he was at the Mayo Clinic in Minnesota, and we arranged for Mom and Dad to visit him. Unbelievably this doctor was also born in Trenton, New Jersey, and attended Trenton High School. He reviewed Dad's lab results and X-rays and confirmed the diagnosis. He agreed with the doctor at Sloan that the disease had no cure, but he said it could be slowed a bit.

There was no hope, only an incessant feeling of helplessness as the biggest trial of my life began.

Dad was anemic and needed to undergo extensive transfusions. At first, they were approximately once a month, and his response was immediate, letting him go into work and return with a bounce in his step. But as the Mayo specialist predicted, the benefits of the transfusions slowed, and Dad started having them weekly. He had deep bruises on both his arms and the backs of his hands that marred his previously clear skin. Just looking at them told me that he was in immense pain, but he never once complained. In the end, the transfusions became so regular and routine that he had a tube inserted in his chest for the process.

I had made several trips to Saint Thomas in the U.S. Virgin Islands with Lou Mercatanti, who was also a sailor. We sailed to several ports together, including Jost Van Dyke in the BVI. In spring 1987, my parents were enjoying their yearly trip to Sanibel Island, off the west coast of Florida. This place was a family favorite dating back to when we were in grammar school. My dad loved to sail. He had taken up the sport later in his life with his great friend Dr. Tony Chiurco and his wife Jane and "baby Eddie," who lived across the street from us on Brookstone Drive. He was an accomplished sailor and had a 47-foot Swan which he docked in Annapolis, MD. He also had a terrific crew of experienced sailors. They entered several races, including the Swan Sardinia Challenge in Sardinia, Italy. Mom and Dad went there, and Dad was a tactician on the boat.

I knew Dad loved sailing, and I arranged to charter a 75-foot Irwin called Drumbeat II, a beautiful sailboat complete with crew and chef for a surprise family trip to the U.S. and British Virgin Islands. I wanted to do something special for Dad. As his health continued to decline, I was having difficulty coping with the deterioration and the inevitable conclusion. I was often unable to sleep and following long days at the office, I sometimes got up in the middle of the night and ran on the country roads till dawn.

For the trip, I had engraved invitations that called it the "Ralph Mason Celebration Tour" in honor of Dad. The invitation said it was a "Thank you for a lifetime of giving." I had the invitation and a descriptive Drumbeat brochure delivered to Mom and Dad.

On the day it arrived, I picked up the phone and Dad was on the other side. He started breaking down in the middle of our conversation and could not finish what he was saying and hung up on me. Mom called back a moment later. She said Dad could not come to the phone; he was overcome with emotion. Hearing my father cry that day made me dread the inevitable a little more. I could not wrap my head around knowing that a person can be reduced to a shell of their former glory by an invisible health anomaly. The question, "Why him?" haunted me day and night.

The trip was wonderful! Dad went with us on many snorkel dives despite his difficulties getting in and out of the water. He always had a huge smile on his face and laughed to his heart's content. In the water, Tom and I took turns swimming with him and supporting him. Dad occasionally drove the boat with the sails upright, glancing over the water on a steep tack. The trip was a celebration of life, with great food and familial cheer. Everyone enjoyed the open-water sailing, especially Dad. No one wanted the trip to end, but it was over far too soon.

Late in 1987, Dad was hospitalized with serious infections arising from his weakened immune system. Two years earlier, I had gotten to know Peter Martin, the founder and President of Symedco, the country's premier medical education firm. Princeton and surrounding areas of New Jersey were a hub of big pharma companies. Peter engaged me to negotiate the buyout of his cofounder, who was leaving the business. The negotiations were contentious and lasted several months, but the final arrangements were fair and both parties went away satisfied. Afterward, Peter retained me to represent the company and to provide business advice and strategic planning.

The many hours Peter and I spent working together led us to become friends, and our young families often gathered for picnics and dinners. When my dad was hospitalized in 1987, Peter joined me in my visits with Dad, and he also provided exceptional insights into the treatment of the disease. One time I arrived to visit Dad at the Princeton Medical Center, where he was the chairman of the board, and I was met by Dr. Carney and by the hospital's head of infectious disease. ID doctors, as they are known, are consulted on drug therapies, including emerging treatments, and they can be somewhat prickly. They often have the most diva-like personalities in any hospital.

This doctor said that to treat my dad's infection, he needed to immediately undergo an intravenous dosage of Claforan, a new third-generation compound. I picked up the phone in Dad's room, called Peter, and told him they were putting my father on this medication.

"Do not let them do that," Peter responded, "It's contraindicated for older patients with weakened immune systems, and it can lead to renal failure."

When I repeated this to the ID physician, he was visibly annoyed. "How do you know that?" he asked. "There's nothing in the medical literature to indicate that side effect."

Peter heard this through the phone and said, "Tell him we are publishing the latest research next month—do not administer the medication."

I returned to my office, confident that Peter's feedback would be followed. That afternoon the ID doctor started the IV, and within hours Dad's kidneys started to fail. Dr. Carney called to tell me he had overruled the specialist and stopped the medication. Fortunately, Dr. Carney had acted quickly enough, because if Dad had been kept on the IV meds for another day, he would not have survived. Instead, he lived for another year, time that meant everything to my family and me.

The next day, I delivered a case of Moët & Chandon White Star Champagne to Peter with a heartfelt thank-you note. With tears in my eyes, I thanked him for saving my dad's life.

Though I had come to accept that Dad would not be with us for much longer, I did not appreciate the persistent gloom and sadness his passing would leave with me. As Dad's health continued to decline, I stopped at his house on most mornings to have coffee with him. Even though he was bedridden and too weak to walk, he always greeted me with a big smile and exclaimed, "It is a beautiful day! I am here for another day!" It was heartbreaking to see him reduced to a helpless man, counting his own steps. Every few mornings, I give him a shave, which seemed to freshen him.

One morning, I asked, "How did you manage to catch this rare illness? It just doesn't make sense." My despair was talking, as I was still struggling to accept his diagnosis. He said he caught it during the war in the Pacific. This was a curious response. I didn't understand. How could he be so certain? He never lost his mental focus, and we frequently talked about matters that I was working on at the firm.

One morning, he said, "I have got something to tell you. I have made a decision that is entirely my own. I am not going back to the hospital for additional transfusions or treatments. I have decided to enter hospice care."

I wanted to maintain calm, and I told him I understood. He had fought for so long and had endured agonizing pain from the illness and the treatments. It made sense he wanted all of it to stop.

As I stood to leave his bedside, Dad commented, "A time will come when you will have alternatives. Don't be hesitant to pursue them."

I was confused and tried to process the devastating decision with advice to move on. Twice over the coming decade, I would understand his message. He was releasing me from the bonds of loyalty to his law firm and from the practice of law.

I walked out of the bedroom that day and gave my mom a hug. I settled myself in my car and broke down in tears; it was all too much for me to handle. I could feel that the end was upon us, but I had no way to change its course.

We celebrated Thanksgiving in 1988 at my dad's house. In keeping with a lifetime of tradition, Mom cooked a big turkey and all the side dishes. Karen and Tom were there, along with Tom's wife Emily. Dad was too sick to come to the dinner table, and his absence was heavy on us.

That night, the phone rang. I could not help but be anxious about whatever awaited me on the other side of the line. Mom was telling me that Dad was resting comfortably. The hospice nurse had visited and given him morphine to help with the pain. A weight was lifted off my shoulders, and I sighed in relief. I spoke briefly to Dad, but he was tired, so we said our goodbyes.

Early the next morning, the phone rang again, and it was Mom. "Dad won't wake up," she said, hysterically. "What should I do?"

I told her to call Dr. Carney, and I jumped in the car and drove to their house.

Several possibilities were running through my mind, but I clutched to the last vestiges of hope. When I reached Dad, he was breathing shallowly, as if the very act of breathing tired him out. Karen, Tom, and Emily arrived soon after, all with red eyes and wild appearances. As we surrounded him in a loose circle and held his hands, he passed away.

Among the items my dad left to me was the Bronze Star Medal he was given for his service during World War II. This is one of the highest honors in the army. I wondered why an officer, and an attorney, would have a Bronze Star? Karen and I started to investigate but found nothing groundbreaking. Dad's service records had been destroyed in a fire, so we didn't have much to begin our search. This was a generation that honored its promises and that included secrecy. I had to ask again why my father had been so sure he contracted this exceptionally rare disease while in the Pacific?

Dad was attached to General Douglas MacArthur's staff and was discharged from the army on March 16, 1946. The first atomic bomb was dropped on Hiroshima on August 6, 1945, with the second bomb three days later on Nagasaki.

Four weeks after the bombings, a small group of reporters and officers on MacArthur's staff were the first Americans to visit Hiroshima and Nagasaki. The destruction and death were staggering, swallowing the whole area in ash and char. It was "hot" with radiation, and apparently, none of the US journalists or officers wore protective gear.

Chicago Daily News reporter George Weller chronicled his observations, but MacArthur's censors blocked the release of Weller's dispatches. They weren't published until 2006.

The Mayo Clinic website notes that exposure to radiation is one of the causes of myelofibrosis. We don't know if Dad was on the flight to visit Hiroshima and Nagasaki, nor can we verify our suspicion that he was because all the records were destroyed, and Dad is no longer with us. Even if he were alive, I doubt he would speak about it. That generation of the military kept its secrets.

With my dad gone, my life had dramatically changed. I recall one night, a few days following his passing, when I broke down in anguish. Shortly after, I started having frequent dreams about him. They began with Dad and I riding in the car and talking while I drove. He would tell me to pull to the side of the road so he could get out. There may be some symbolism in him asking me to let him out of the car, but I never asked anyone to interpret that. The dreams were always vivid, painted in the brightest colors. I experienced forgotten fragrances and summer breezes, yet I could not shake off the feelings of deep sadness they invoked in me. Close friends and family were a source of consolation, but I needed to heal on my own.

A couple of months later, I was on a business trip to Spain, helping out my good friend and client Peter Martin on whose board of directors I was a member. One evening following the typical Spanish dinner that ends after midnight, I returned exhausted to my hotel room and fell to sleep. That night, I had the most remarkable dream of my life. I was a young boy, perhaps six years old, and I entered the old location of the law offices at 201 Nassau Street in Princeton. The office had a long hallway that ran the entire right side of the building. The hallway turned left at the end of the offices. As I entered, I was standing in what seemed to be a typical workday; attorneys and staff were hustling about, people were attending to clients and going through files.

Looking through the many legs of moving people, I saw Dad farther down the hall. I started to yell for him, "Dad, I am coming." As I ran down the hallway, I started aging and getting taller. I reached the end to turn left, following him and saw that I was an adult and running hard. I made the left turn, and there he was, waiting for me. I practically ran into him and was astonished that we were the same age as we stood facing each other. He had a stern look on his face when he asked, "Why are you doing this? I am here whenever you need me."

I woke up with a start, drenched in sweat and my emotions, but somehow a sense of calm had descended on me. The pain had abated, giving me an opportunity to look at the world from a new perspective. It was time for me to move on. I had come to realize that my father was always there for me whenever I needed him.

I just needed to reach out to him in my memories and embrace his presence. He has been gone for more than 30 years, but we still talk from time to time, and he is here with me.

Chapter 5

A New Law Firm

In 1985, I was introduced to Kenneth Taylor by the executive management of Merrill Lynch. He would become my close friend and mentor for many decades. I remember him as a man sporting square-rimmed glasses and a kind smile. He wore impressively tailored suits with matching ties, but it was his unruly curls that made him approachable. His appearance was a sharp contrast between an important-looking businessman and an amiable professor.

In the late 1970s and early 1980s, Ken played a consequential role in American history while serving as Canada's ambassador to Iran. He was sent to Tehran in 1977 by the Canadian prime minister after some years as the head of the Trade Commissioner Service. Two years later, on November 4, 1979, the world was shocked when the American embassy in Tehran was stormed and seized by Iranian students who held hostage more than 50 Americans. This brazen attack and kidnapping was a violation of international law as well as diplomatic customs that had been honored for centuries.

Six members of the embassy staff managed to avoid capture and got out of the building without anyone knowing it. Fleeing through the streets of Tehran, they sought shelter at the embassies of several US allies, only to be turned away. Eventually, they reached the Canadian embassy and Ambassador Ken Taylor. Without consulting his Home Office, Ken and his wife Pat immediately offered their residence as shelter to the shaken American staff. Meanwhile, the international media was focused exclusively on the personnel captured inside the American embassy and didn't notice that six were unaccounted for.

American television audiences followed the events unfolding in Tehran through nightly reports by Ted Koppel on his program Nightline. Koppel opened each segment with a countdown of the days in captivity. His show became mandatory viewing across the United States, as American citizens were frustrated and unnerved by the kidnappings.

Jean Pelletier, the Washington correspondent for Montreal's La Presse, noted that the number of staff being reported as hostages did not match the number inside the embassy at the time of the seizure. When Pelletier contacted the US State Department, he was asked to meet a representative at a restaurant.

Ken and Pat described for me what happened during these days a number of times over the years. According to Ken, Pelletier was told that he was correct: six staffers were not among the hostages. But he was also told, "If you break the story, their lives will be in danger. If you sit on the story, you will get an exclusive interview when they are released."

Pelletier sat on the most explosive story of 1979 and 1980.

After the seizure of the embassy, American reporters were expelled from Iran, but ABC News was fortunate that one of their premier journalists, Peter Jennings, was Canadian, and he could get into this fundamentalist Muslim country. Jennings was also a good friend of Ken's, and while in Tehran, he visited Ken and Pat. In those early days of the hostage crisis, when Jennings came by, the six US embassy staffers climbed the stairs to the attic where they wouldn't be spotted. Jennings joked later that the best story of his career had been just a few feet above his head.

Ken and everyone knew the six couldn't stay in the Canadian embassy for long without getting caught, and early in 1980 a plan was devised for them to fly out of Iran. The US State Department supplied passport photos to the Home Office in Canada; they were inserted into Canadian passports, which, along with visas, were forwarded to Ken via diplomatic pouch. The Iranians, fearful of western rescue attempts and insertion of agents, had begun changing the color of immigration stamps and signatures to catch forgeries. The passports and paperwork arrived just a few days before the staffers were scheduled to fly out of Tehran. Embassy personnel noted that a misunderstanding of the Iranian calendar had caused the dates on the visas to indicate that they had been issued sometime in the future. The entry dates reflected the proposed exit date. At their kitchen table, Ken and Pat fixed the error by forging each already-forged passport to reflect the correct date and the proper color of the day for Iranian Customs and Immigration inspectors. They never told the staff about any of this, fearful that anxieties would be further inflamed.

As the six were nearing the day when they would go to the airport, Ken and Pat had still not been given tickets for the travel out of Iran. In the end, Pat purchased the reservations on her personal American Express card.

The 2012 movie *Argo* starring Ben Affleck, was a highly fictionalized version of the six staffers and how they escaped from Iran. It won the Academy Award for Best Picture and was dubbed a "historical drama," but it was far from a factual recounting. It is true the CIA developed the cover story that the staffers were from a Canadian documentary film company to explain why they were in Iran and as Canadian citizens could now leave. But the attribution of slick CIA competence and attention to every detail was inaccurate.

The six embassy staffers made it to the west on January 27, 1980. When news of Ken's heroism in helping them get out of Iran became public, he was hailed as a hero and was awarded the Congressional Gold Medal, which is "bestowed by the United States Congress as its highest expression of national recognition for distinguished achievements and contributions."

Ambassador Kenneth Taylor New York. 1987

I was honored to get to know Ken. When we first met, he was the senior vice president of international business at RJR Nabisco, where he worked closely with fellow Canadian Ross Johnson. (Ross would be played by James Garner in the 1993 HBO movie *Barbarians at the Gate*, based on the book about the company's subsequent sale to private equity firm KKR, at the time the largest buyout in history.)

I introduced Ken to several of my clients, including Peter Martin, the founder and President of Symedco, the preeminent medical education company in North America. Peter had also played a life-saving role in the last year of my dad's life. Ken's wife Pat was a scientist at the New York Blood Center and was involved in pioneering AIDS research. Peter and I often had dinners with Ken and Pat in New York and in New Jersey, and Peter and Pat developed a close professional relationship. At my suggestion, Ken joined the board of directors at Symedco, where I was already a member. He frequently invited me to join him on trips to Toronto, where I met many members of the Canadian diplomatic corps and leaders of industry and commerce.

In 1987, Ken and I worked together on the US Olympic Committee, Wall Street Division, and we put together a fundraiser for the US Olympic teams that would be competing at the winter games the next year in Calgary. We arranged to have the event take place on the American Stock Exchange floor. At the time, it was the largest single fundraiser in US Olympic history. More than 50 Olympians attended, along with members of the New York Rangers hockey team and the New York Knicks basketball team.

No one had ever used the American Stock Exchange building for fundraising. I chartered a bus and brought up my law partners and Hobson's choice of clients. We had live music, open bars, and lots of food—all donated by restaurants and bars. Even the security was donated. Every dollar raised from the event went directly to the US Olympic community. It was indeed the social event of the summer of 1987 in New York.

My path with Ken converged again when he asked me to negotiate his severance with Nabisco. What started as a professional association soon catapulted into a friendship banking on trust and understanding. I frequented his residence in Metropolitan Tower, next to Carnegie Hall in New York, for many business and friendly dinners when we enjoyed delicious food and esoteric conversations along with his wife Pat. More often than not, my interests aligned with Ken, giving us opportunities to spend more time together. Consequently, we went on numerous business trips to a host of countries and cities, including Mexico City, Paris, London, Moscow, Toronto, and Rio. My association with Ken led me to meet Don Trump, Henry Kissinger, Peter Jennings, Christopher Plummer, and Ken's college roommate, Donald Sutherland.

When Ken was moving out of his offices at Nabisco, an incident occurred that led to an incommensurable historical loss. The janitorial staff assisting with his move threw out an extensive collection of Ken's diplomatic notes and other original material. Ken's assistant, Maria, had placed signs indicating that this was his extensive collection of diplomatic notes and other important original material, and that it was not to be removed. Unfortunately, the janitorial staff assisting with the move could not read English, and while Ken was out for lunch, they threw out everything.

Maria returned to the office from her lunch and discovered the catastrophe of the missing records and called me. She was hysterical and in tears and could barely explain the situation to me. I called the building management, and they immediately went to work to locate the missing documents and folios.

By this time, the papers were already in a public landfill. Overnight and with help from anyone we could think of, we could not retrieve the papers. Later in the afternoon, Ken called, still in the dark about what had happened and why Maria was so upset. I told him about the mishap and the efforts we'd taken to find the missing documents.

Ken was cautious with his dealings. He reassured me in his ever-patient and calm manner that I shouldn't burden myself with this anymore. I filed a claim against the building and staff and secured a financial recovery that Ken appreciated. But the money was not commensurate with the loss.

Law firms annually review each attorney's billable hours, new matters originated, and revenue developed. My dad's firm maintained a significant municipal law practice, but the hourly rates for that work were modest compared to the rates for Dad's services related to trusts and estate planning. The municipal law practice rates were also much lower than what I was commanding in a rapidly growing commercial practice. By 1985, my services had expanded, and I had hired two additional attorneys to work with me and to serve my clients' business needs. I also utilized several of the firm's litigators to represent my clients in complex commercial litigations and that helped support the family law and municipal work. As my points in the profits grew each year, my income was among the top three or four attorneys in the firm.

All the firm's revenues were combined, but careful records were kept of which attorney had originated each piece of business. After expenses were paid, including secretarial support, net profits were paid to the partners according to their "points" or profit percentages. The points allocations were reviewed and adjusted during a meeting at the start of each year, based on each lawyer's individual metrics from the prior year. This meeting was generally calm, and Dad, who often diminished his own allocation to bridge differences, engineered a collegial consensus.

My corporate practice, with the additional billing power of three lawyers at rates three times that of the municipal lawyers, became the firm's highest-grossing segment. I sensed a rising resentment among the municipal and family practice lawyers. As my dad's health declined, his hours at work decreased. At a weekly meeting in late spring of 1988, several partners voiced their desire to reduce Dad's points as his hours had declined. I was incensed and reacted with amazement at their proposal, using colorful and inflammatory rhetoric. I noted that many of them had gained points over the years due to Dad's generosity and that the firm had never adjusted points during the year. A schism had formed that would never be repaired.

Following Dad's death in November 1988, and despite the overwhelming sadness, or perhaps because of it, I poured myself into growing my practice even more. New clients were referred regularly. Existing client needs and acquisitions were also expanding. In the meantime, tensions at the firm did not diminish. Early in the fall of 1990, I knew I had to depart. After an intense partner meeting, I spoke with two close friends and fellow corporate lawyers who worked with me, and we all agreed that the time had arrived to leave the firm founded by my dad more than 45 years ago. Together we would form our own law firm.

In early November 1990, I dropped into Gordon Griffin's office and gave him the news that I was leaving. He was sad but not surprised, and he noted the significant difference between my practice specialty and that of the firm's other members. Gordon had been Dad's oldest partner, and I had known him my entire life. I suggested to Gordon that a two- to three-month disengagement was sensible to avoid any disruptions in client services. Under our partnership agreement, I retained no rights to any partnership distributions following my departure, including payments for work already billed or for work in process. Later that evening, I received a call from another partner who said my resignation was accepted. Effective immediately. The acceptance of my resignation the day I offered it halted all my partner distributions and compensation.

By offering to stay on for several months to work out details, I had left myself completely vulnerable, and the result was an immediate cutoff of all income. This was something I would never have permitted a client to do.

I was not the only one leaving the firm, and my corporate partners who were departing with me gathered at my home. Ellen was eight and a half months pregnant, and understandably, her first question was whether we still had medical insurance.

Over the next two days, with little (or no) sleep, I hammered out arrangements for the new firm. We had no office, no phones, and no secretarial support. Nothing. I called my good friend and former legal mentor Richard Altman, who was now the managing partner of another firm. Richard had joined Tom, Dave, and me on several of our summer hikes in North Carolina and Vermont. He immediately offered me and my partners office space, along with the secretarial and phone services at his firm. He refused any offer of payment.

Long-settled legal practice rules state that clients have the exclusive right to determine who will represent them. That evening, without a secretary, I set to work handwriting representation letters to our key clients. I had to prepare them all by hand in triplicate because one copy would be given to the old firm, another was for the new firm, and the final copy was for the client. I did not have a copy machine.

Over the next week, more than 150 clients, including major banks, insurance companies, manufacturers, and pharma businesses, executed my handwritten transfer notices. Not one of our clients asked to stay with the old firm.

While I was working out of Richard's office, I received a call from a local news reporter. "I hear that you've left your father's firm," she said. "What led to this separation and do you have any comments?" I was stunned and responded, "It must be a slow news day."

The reporter said she already had comments from a representative of my dad's firm but declined to tell me what they were. I recalled my dad's advice and decided to keep to the high road and simply noted that the new firm would be devoted exclusively to commercial and transactional practice.

I was working all hours to set up the new firm, but sometimes life tells you to stop what you're doing because something really important is happening. On November 18, 1990, two years after Ellen and I got married, we were blessed with a beautiful baby boy, Taylor. He was born at Princeton Hospital, the same place where my mom and Uncle Tim were born. Karen, Tom, and I were born there as well. I would say something about the circle of life and everything coming back to a place where we started, but it really was about all of us living in the same town for years. It was home, and it was where we belonged.

I recall the time leading up to Taylor's birth and the reflections everyone shared with me, and I find myself overwhelmed with nostalgia. I was told that life would never be the same after I held that fragile bundle of limbs in my embrace, and they were right.

Moments after Taylor was born, I could not contain my emotions. I called my mother, and we both cried over the phone just thinking about the new life and the one we had lost, Dad. Several hours later, my mom, Karen, Tom, Emily, and I went to the Yankee Doodle Tap Room at the Nassau Inn for a brief celebration. It was nothing remarkable, but it was with family, so it was warmth, longing, and memories. There was a tradition in the Tap Room of etching initials and full names into the table tops there. That day, I carved Taylor's initials into a table, thinking about my dad, Pappy, and their legacy. In memory of Pappy, Taylor's middle name is Harris, so carving his initials meant something symbolic for me at the time. (A number of years ago, they covered the tabletops with glass, preserving generations of inscribers, including my carving on the day of Taylor's birth in 1990.)

I had seen what an exceptional mother Ellen was with Stevie and Chris, and it was not surprising for me to see her be the same with Taylor. She knew everyone's schedule in the house and catered to my work obligations, making it easy for me to earn a living. How she managed all that remains a mystery to me.

During that time, I had a lot on my plate getting the new firm going, but whenever I was home, I carried my little guy around the house. He and I became fast friends, and soon the line between parenting and friendship was blurred, but I never forgot my obligations as a father. Taylor knew who he was talking to even when we were fooling around in the house like kids. I can go as far as to say that he was attached to my hip, aligning his schedule with mine. He often napped with me when I returned from early-morning hockey games and practices with Chris and Stevie. One of his favorite things to do was ride with me on my tractor to cut the grass, which I had done with my dad 40 years earlier on the same lawn. That was a circle of life—my childhood coming back to me through Taylor.

Taylor had a unique way of demanding things that was adorable and slightly pressuring. In the winter, he stumbled into the kitchen carrying the old running shoes I put on to work outside, and he yelled "tractor!" hugging my legs with his tiny hands. He was always prepared for an adventure and was never shy about pursuing me to heed his demands. He was sneaky; I will give him that.

I made arrangements for office space for our new firm in Carnegie Center, a beautiful and new office campus managed by my good friend Bill King. He and I had served together for several years on the boards of the Princeton YMCA and the Hun School of Princeton. Bill walked me over to one of his brand-new buildings, took me inside, and asked, "Will this do?" Once again, another surprise—Bill refused any upfront payment and told me to let him know when the new firm could start paying rent.

Matters took off from there. The AT&T representative who had taken care of me at Dad's office set us up with phones and extra lines—no charges, he said, "start paying when you can." The Xerox representative did the same, and this was at a time when high-end copiers cost more than half a million dollars. Several secretaries from the old firm called and asked if they could join us. We were up and running in days. Several major clients offered to pay us months in advance to help with expenses.

The outpouring of generosity and support was humbling. We were ready to win.

As the new law firm was coming together in November, Kevin Briody, one of my partners who worked with me at my dad's firm, introduced us to two exceptional commercial lawyers he had worked with previously. We invited these attorneys—Tom Gallagher and John Butler—to join us, and they brought with them an exceptional book of clients that was complementary to mine.

We also brought in Phil Colicchio, a terrific corporate litigator, and the firm's growth was meteoric. We were constantly taking on new accounts, and our existing clients kept us busy with multiple acquisitions. We were creating so much work product to support the clients that our secretarial staff was always busy and occasionally overwhelmed. We scheduled a second secretarial shift during the early evening to take over the computers and workstations. Eventually, we had secretarial assistance 24 hours a day, including most weekends. This was unheard of at the time.

Each year the New Jersey Law Journal does a survey of partner and associate compensation for the state of New Jersey. Although we never agreed to share our partnership compensation for publication, the information proudly provided by the largest commercial firms in the state revealed that we were the highest-compensated attorneys in New Jersey. Our practice also began to extend outside of New Jersey, and we took office space in New York and Philadelphia.

On January 3, 1993, a little more than two years after Taylor's birth, Ellen and I were blessed with a baby girl we named Charlotte. She was cheerful, radiant, and the most beautiful thing I had ever seen. All of Charlotte's nicknames are related to her bright personality, and even now, she lives up to them.

Later in the year after she was born, we had a christening of Taylor and Charlotte at our church in Lawrenceville. It was a joyous event, attended by family and friends, including Ken and Pat Taylor.

I started reading bedtime stories to both of my youngest kids when they were just infants. Their rooms became a kind of a mini theatre because I tried changing my voice to fit each of the characters in the stories. As they got a little older, the one-man show evolved into group narratives, where typically I started and then passed the tale to Taylor, who in turn did the same to Charlotte. Silly mistakes were made that led to infectious laughter and tickling attacks. It was innocent fun, and a memorable part of parenting.

By the time Chris entered junior high school, we were traveling to play hockey against elite teams in New Jersey, New York, and Pennsylvania. The stakes were high as he moved up the ladder, and Ellen and I knew Chris needed training, so we provided him with the best. We sent him to a hockey camp in the summer at Cornell University and to a professional camp run by the NHL North Stars team in Minnesota.

As he entered high school, top prep schools tried to recruit him to play for their teams. Chris and I maintained a rigorous schedule of practice several nights a week, and he played more than 80 games a season, including high school contests.

My corporate practice in New York, New Jersey, and London grew significantly in the early 1990s. Relationships with executives at Merrill Lynch and several major US companies led to a host of new opportunities. Around that time, I met Paul Inderbitzin, the CEO of American Re-insurance. Am Re (as it was known) was the largest reinsurance company in the United States, and they relocated to Princeton.

Paul was a contemporary, and he had two kids at the Hun School where I was chairman of the board of trustees. Paul and I became great friends, and he and his wife Carol joined Ellen and me regularly for dinners together. They invited us to join them for summer vacations at their home on one of the New York Finger Lakes, and we also vacationed with them in Palm Desert.

Am Re had been acquired from Aetna in 1992 by Kohlberg Kravis Roberts & Co.—better known as KKR, a pioneer in private equity, which had bought Nabisco. In 1993, Paul asked me to head up a potential investment opportunity, the acquisition of a bank for them in Prague, a city I had never visited. After the Berlin Wall came down in late 1989, former Soviet nations, like the Czech Republic, began opening their industries, including banks, for foreign investment. Paul knew I'd begun to travel extensively to London and that I represented two London-based banks: Barclays Bank and National Westminster Bank.

Over the next 18 months, I made ten or more trips to Prague. The city is amazing. Many nights, I walked the quiet streets until late, absorbing the ambiance and stunning architecture. Prague is one of the only major cities in Eastern Europe that was not bombed in World War II, and its historical treasures are still there to be seen. I also discovered in Prague an investment fervor I had never seen previously. The average citizen under Soviet rule had never invested in companies, but now taxi drivers and hotel clerks were glued to the financial sections and stock reports in their newspapers. It was amazing.

I had a number of meetings with the bankers who were preparing to hold their first shareholder meeting. They had arranged for it to take place in a large conference room at a hotel. Several days in advance, their phone lines were jammed with shareholders who wanted to attend, and quickly they realized the room they had booked might not be large enough. They first moved to a ballroom and finally ended up in a soccer stadium as some 50,000 shareholders—many with only one share of stock—showed up to participate. This was the birth of a new era of capitalism, and I was there to see it.

Sometime in 1995, Bill Schreyer, the CEO and Chairman of Merrill Lynch, asked me to attend a meeting for him in Washington, DC, where I would meet Lamar Alexander, the senator from Tennessee who was considering entering the 1996 primaries to become the Republican nominee during the campaign for president that year. Also at the meeting were former Tennessee senator Howard Baker and Senator Fred Thompson of Tennessee. Lamar was witty and exceptionally knowledgeable of business and economics. He told me how he had successfully coaxed the Japanese to build their first US-based plant in Tennessee, which was the first US car facility outside Detroit. The whole afternoon was engaging, and everyone there encouraged Lamar to run.

I hadn't thought that one of the reasons I was there was to be observed and screened as a potential Republican candidate for office, but that must have been true. Back in Princeton, I met with Bill and told him I was excited to support Lamar's campaign. I hosted a reception for Lamar at the Princeton Hyatt Regency and invited at least 100 corporate clients, family, and friends, including Bill. Lamar captivated the crowd with his folksy charm and stories.

After the reception, Ellen told Lamar how impressive he was, but she suggested that he needed to "up" his wardrobe if he hoped to capture northeastern voters. He laughed and told her he totally agreed with her assessment.

Several weeks later, I attended a second fundraiser for Lamar at the Hyatt Regency in New Brunswick. I had contributed and bought a table, and the event drew a crowd of more than a thousand people. I was walking through the crowd and talking with a lot of people, when I felt a tap on the shoulder.

"Do you have a moment to meet with Bill?" the person asked.

I found Bill in a private conference room with five or ten others. He asked me to sit down. "Would you consider being a candidate in 1997 for governor of the state of New Jersey as an initial step to national office? We have all campaign costs covered."

"Bill," I responded, politely, "I could never afford the cut in pay, with four kids in private schools."

I heard later that Paul Inderbitzin supported and encouraged my candidacy, as did Ken Taylor. Everyone knew about this but me. I declined their offer, but I was humbled by it and the support from such exceptional men whom I respected.

Lamar Alexander ran for president in 1996 and finished third in the Iowa caucuses and third in the New Hampshire primary, but he dropped out before Super Tuesday. The Republican Party chose old-guard candidate Bob Dole as their nominee, and Bill Clinton was reelected to a second term as president of the United States. We learned several months later that the Clinton campaign's greatest fear had been that Lamar would emerge as the Republican nominee.

In 1996, the Summer Olympics were held in Atlanta, GA, and the once-proud US boxing team was outmatched at most weight divisions. Shortly after the closing ceremony, Ken Taylor called me at the office. He was just back from Kazakhstan, where he was working on a Skylink matter.

"Rip, Vassiliy Jirov, a young Kazak boxer, won the Olympic gold medal. He was also voted the best boxer at the games. The same award was won by Muhammad Ali in Rome. He is turning pro and needs representation. I need for you to be his lawyer. Tonight, we are flying to Vegas, where you can negotiate his contract with Bob Arum."

"Ken," I said, stunned. "You know I love boxing, but I know nothing about boxing contracts."

"You will be fine," he said. "I know Bob well. He wants this fighter. You can figure it out on site."

I met my new client and his "crew" of trainers and coaches on the flight to Vegas that night. The next morning a car sent by Bob Arum was waiting at the hotel to pick us up. Vassiliy and his entourage would join us later.

Bob enthusiastically greeted me at his office, and we chatted over coffee. I learned that prior to his legendary career as a boxing promoter, he had prosecuted high-profile cases as a US attorney. His walls were covered with photographs of legends he had managed in the past, among them Muhammad Ali, George Foreman, Roberto Duran, Sugar Ray Leonard, and Joe Frazier. As a youngster, I had watched boxing on Friday nights with my dad on the small black-and-white TV. In later years, I went to Madison Square Garden to see Muhammad Ali, Larry Holmes, Roberto Durán, Carlos Palomino, and others fight. I was in Bob's office to represent my client, and I had to keep myself from being overwhelmed in the presence of boxing royalty.

When Vassiliy arrived, we had a quick lunch and headed to the

Top Rank gym. Bob wanted to impress Vassiliy with the gym. He asked me to ride with him, while Ken and the others climbed into a fleet of limos. Arriving at the building, I asked Bob, "What are your thoughts on Vassiliy as a pro?"

Bob pointed to one of the rings where an incredibly in-shape fighter was sparing. "See that guy, Rip. He is the world champion light heavyweight. Your guy would destroy him today wearing his suit and tie."

I was stunned. The leap from amateur to pro was big. Three rounds of fights are replaced with 12 rounds of incredible exertion and physical challenge.

That evening Bob hosted an exceptional dinner, and as he departed, he leaned over and said, "I will meet you and the guys at the office tomorrow, and we'll hammer out the contract."

I had a fitful night back in my hotel room because I was not experienced in these types of agreements. In the morning, as we were arriving back at the Top Rank office, a solution came to mind.

Bob was all business, surrounded by his lawyers, assistants, and staff on one side of a large conference room table. On the other side, Ken was seated to my left and Vassiliy was on the other side.

"Okay, Rip, how would you like to proceed?" Bob asked, starting us off.

"Bob, first let me thank you for the hospitality. As I mentioned the other day, I am not experienced with these agreements. Who would you say is your top fighter today?"

Without a moment of hesitation, Bob replied, "Oscar De La Hoya." De La Hoya was known as the golden boy.

"Bob, I would like Vassiliy to have Oscar's contract. Then we can negotiate the price."

Bob's lawyers were stunned and erupted with derision and some colorful language. Bob started to smile at me. "Give Rip Oscar's contract," he said to his attorneys. "We can get this put to bed before lunch."

The lawyers could not believe what they were hearing, but after some more grumbling, the De La Hoya contract appeared at last. A short while later, Bob and I were shaking hands and laughing. A translator had to explain what had just happened to the Kazaks with Vassiliy, but I was hailed as a hero with salutations that I could not understand. Ken was smiling broadly as we all headed to lunch.

In 1996, KKR decided to explore the sale of American Reinsurance. Bankers were engaged, and several large competitors were approached to assess interest. While interest abounded, the bankers failed to conclude a transaction. Paul and I met at Chez Odette, a restaurant in New Hope, PA, to discuss the situation, and we determined that it was time to ask KKR to have their management speak directly to several candidate buyers. KKR agreed, and these discussions lead quickly to a $3.3 billion transaction to sell American Re to Munich Re—the largest reinsurance company globally.

Paul and I were jubilant. This would be the best return on investment for any KKR deal in history. A central part of the closing was for executive management to enter into new agreements and to continue to operate American Re. Paul asked me to handle the negotiations with the Germans. My lifelong friend Steve Bachelder was one of the premier executive compensation specialists in the country. He joined me, and we mapped out a proposed structure that included exceptional tax advantages for the management.

The day arrived for our negotiation of the deal terms, and Steve and I boarded the train to New York at the Princeton Junction train station. I purchased The Wall Street Journal for the ride into the city, as I always did. Unbelievably, the article in the center of the front page was about the American Re sale to Munich Re. It focused extensively on the American Re management team as the best in the business and said this was among the top reasons in support of the deal.

We reached the law offices of Munich Re's attorneys and were ushered into a large conference room. Several members of Munich Re's management team were there, along with four or five lawyers, bankers, and accountants. They were quiet and a bit sullen. Steve and I were seated across from them. I decided not to open my briefcase with the extensive documentation we had assembled for the negotiations. Instead, I asked how many of them had read the Wall Street Journal that morning. They looked quizzical, and I pushed my copy across the table to their lead negotiator and suggested they read it while Steve and I waited outside.

Several minutes later we came back inside, and I suggested we dispense with their opening position and move to the deal they were prepared to accept as a fallback. There was some nervous laughter.

Three point three billion dollars sat in the balance. Within an hour, it was over. We shook hands on an exceptional structure and a deal for the current management team to stay on and run the company.

I called Paul from the lobby. He was laughing and offering me congratulations. I called KKR and let them know that this final piece was completed and the sale could now go through. They were delighted.

My practice in London was also growing rapidly. One of my clients, Vincent Tchenguiz, provided me with an opulent office on Curzon Street in the tony Mayfair district. Among my US-based clients, including the wholly owned subsidiaries of National Westminster Bank and Barclays Bank, many have London-based operations. My college roommate Charlie Cavness was the CEO of an oil and gas exploration firm. He and I met several times in London for meetings with potential business partners. On these trips, we managed to find some time to visit historical sites around that city, including Hampton Court—the home of Henry VIII.

In 1996, Vincent called and let me know they wanted to acquire a London-based direct-selling business and asked me to look into it. They also needed help finding an operating executive. I was having lunch that day in New York with the former president of Schick, and he asked me what I was working on. I told him about the inquiry from London, and he suggested I call a friend of his, the former CEO of Tupperware. When I reached my New York office after lunch, I found a message to call to Ron Clark, the president of Mary Kay Europe. He lived in London, and his office was 100 yards from mine on Curzon Street. Ron and I agreed to meet in London the next day. I took the overnight flight out of JFK.

In Ron's office the next morning, I told him about the business Vincent was interested in. Ron pulled out an enormous file and dropped it on his desk. "Help yourself," he said, "we have spent some time looking at the company and have decided to pass."

Our discussion quickly moved to Ron's career in direct sales. He was the former president of Avon USA, where he had worked for 30 years. He was also the head of Avon Latin America. Ron was a Renaissance man—fluent in several languages, an MBA from Thunderbird, Army Ranger, paratrooper, and former boxer. He fought as an amateur in Madison Square Garden under another name (because he knew his mother would not approve).

We hit it off immediately. "Ron, would you be interested in a larger transaction?" I asked.

"What do you have in mind, Rip?" he responded. "Would you like to try and buy Mary Kay?"

Ron laughed, "That would be a very big check."

I suggested that KKR might have an interest and asked if he would travel with me to New York to meet with Henry Kravis. Ron was stunned. "You know Henry?" he asked.

I nodded in the affirmative and described the transactions I had worked on with KKR.

Two days later, Ron and I were in New York, sitting in Henry's office. As I had hoped, Henry was taken with Ron, who presented a detailed overview of Mark Kay operations, including their accelerating business in Russia. Several hours later, Henry turned to me and said, "Rip, I would like to do this deal. Please get it going."

Ron and I departed, and there had been abundant laughter among all of us. Literally, we had the checkbook. It was time to go to work. Within days, Ron was in touch with Mary Kay's family and with John Rochon, the company's CEO. Despite initial resistance, there seemed to be an interest in an exploratory discussion. They recognized that KKR had the financial capacity to complete a multi-billion-dollar transaction.

Several weeks later, as we were preparing for a meeting, we learned Mary Kay Ash, who had founded the company, had had a stroke and her condition was unknown. All discussions were put on indefinite hold.

As several months passed, into 1997, without follow-up from the people at Mary Kay, Ron and I decided to look for another transaction. He suggested we investigate Jafra Cosmetics, a company that had been owned by Gillette for 25 years. Jafra was a multilevel direct seller of cosmetics with operations in 16 countries throughout Europe and Latin America. Their largest business was in Mexico, with the United States serving as the headquarters and the second largest business unit. Gillette had been approached for years to sell the business but had always refused any overtures.

In a bit of luck around this time, Gillette had entered into an agreement to buy Duracell from KKR. This was a stock deal, and it meant that KKR emerged as one of the largest owners of Gillette stock. I meet with Henry Kravis, who as part of the deal would go on the Gillette board of directors, and asked if he could ask Gillette's CEO and chairman if they would consider selling Jafra. Henry was told that Gillette liked the long-held Jafra business and was not interested in a sale. Even so, Gillette's chairman arranged for me to meet with someone in his office to explore the matter.

In my efforts to convince Gillette to consider a sale of Jafra, I noted in calls and meetings that Jafra was the only nonretail brand in their portfolio, and it was strategically different from their other holdings. Gillette had recently taken on significant corporate debt, and I pointed out to them that a cash sale of Jafra would help reduce the outstanding borrowing base. Despite their initial resistance, ongoing calls ultimately led Gillette to explore a possible sale of Jafra. Looking back on it in later years, I believe that a key reason they agreed to sell was to stop me from calling the chairman's office.

They were properly concerned with confidentiality because they maintained a large sales force of independent contractors who might depart and join other network businesses if word of a sale leaked. This concern worked to our advantage, making it a limited sale process, with only three parties, including KKR, invited to engage with management to learn about the company. All meetings with Jafra executive management were held off-site and after normal business hours, when employees had left in order to limit the risk of a leak. We were prohibited from touring the facilities or attending field events. First bids were due within a matter of weeks.

I worked closely with Perry Golkin at KKR, whom I had first met when we worked on the American Re sale, to investigate everything we needed to know about Jafra before entering the bidding process to acquire the company.

Gillette retained Merrill Lynch to act as their banker for the sale. Ray McGuire, who many years later in 2021 ran unsuccessfully for mayor of New York City, headed the Merrill team. Ray and I worked closely together as he scripted the management meetings and diligence process. We were off to a good start at our first meeting, because he knew of my long history with the CEO and chairman at Merrill.

Following several meetings in California, the first round of bids was required. We submitted a proposal that moved us into the second round, providing great access to company's facilities and personnel. The second round of bids was also successful, and we advanced to the final round with pricing guidance from Merrill. In the interim, I befriended the Gillette CFO and gained important insights.

In preparation for the final bid, we traveled to Jafra operations in Mexico City, Munich, Milan, Vienna, and other cities. It was now fall 1997, and the final bid was due in 45 days. It was an exhausting schedule as Ron and I together with our partner Gonzalo Rubio worked seven days a week in hotels and on airplanes, refining our financial and strategic plans. Living out of suitcases with little rest, it was essential that we completed our local market reviews before the bid submission date. Merrill imposed customary rigor on both bidders to provide a level playing field. Delays or missed dates would lead to dismissal from the sales process.

With KKR, we agreed to submit a final all-cash bid of $200 million on the stipulated due date. On the evening prior to the bid, after I had finished dinner with my family, Perry called me at home. I could tell he was agitated. Months of work by him and his team, along with Ron Clark, Gonzalo Rubio, and me, had gone into the review of the company, the development of growth strategies, and the forecasts.

"Rip, as you are aware, final bids are due tomorrow at noon," Perry said. "I am sorry to report that KKR will not be proceeding with the bid."

I was floored. This was completely unanticipated. Perry believed in the deal and the new management opportunities. As he explained, this was a last-minute internal decision at KKR because they were working simultaneously on several larger deals and felt they could not cover all of it.

I asked Perry to hold off until the next morning at 10:00 a.m. before notifying Merrill Lynch of their decision. Perry readily agreed but said, "Rip, where are you going to find $200 million overnight?"

Chapter 6

Jafra

After the call from Perry Golkin, I called Brian Finn, a former senior lender at Credit Suisse in New York, who was Mary Kay's banker and who had recently left the bank and joined CD&R, another New York–based private equity firm. After I explained that a final bid was required in just a few hours, I began faxing our 100page investment memo to him. Brian and I were on the phone for hours that night, and then he had calls to make with his partners at CD&R.

After 2:00 a.m., Brian called. "Rip, we are interested," he said. "This is a big ask at the final hour, but we will submit a $200 million bid on behalf of your team in the morning."

The next morning, I contacted Ray McGuire, who was on his way to his office at Merrill. "Ray, KKR will not be proceeding with a final bid," I said. "CD&R has agreed to partner with management and will be submitting a full price offer by noon today."

Ray was stunned and delighted. He did not inquire why KKR had declined to proceed. He knew the partners of CD&R and knew about their successful history of acquiring divisions of larger businesses, including their recent purchase of Lexmark, the printing division of IBM. CD&R's experience in this form of specialized purchase would be seen as a positive development and would assist in successfully completing the transaction.

A few hours later, I received a call from Brian, along with several of his CD&R partners. One of them said, "We just spoke to Brian and have submitted our joint $200 million bid with your new management partners."

In keeping with standard deal protocols, Ray called Brian late that afternoon and said, "I'm pleased to advise that Gillette has accepted your offer."

This was good news, but now that we had successfully won the bid to purchase Jafra, additional and significant obstacles remained before we could buy the company. Gillette was a public company, and a number of regulatory applications were required in the United States and foreign countries. Merrill Lynch also followed the bidding process and provided a standard form of purchase agreement. To close our financing of the transaction, we needed an independent and stand-alone audit of the Jafra financial results.

The sprint was now on with documentation, confirmatory diligence, and financing arrangements, and we also needed to revisit the local Jafra markets. Within days of learning that we won the bid, I traveled with David Novak, Don Gogel, and Tom Ireland of CD&R to Boston, the home city of Gillette. CD&R's New York lawyers met us at the offices of Ropes & Gray, attorneys for Gillette. Merrill sent several representatives, and we were joined by Gillette's CFO, whom I had befriended during the earlier management presentations. This relationship proved to be a key element in the purchase.

We negotiated in a large conference room, with at least 20 people there. Key negotiators were at the table, and support teams sat in chairs along the walls. Each side did their initial posturing and put forth their "bottom-line" expectancies. I was well versed in these protocols and knew that "bottom lines" were seldom that.

Gillette presented their position first, our side rebutted, and everyone retired to private conference rooms. An hour later, we reengaged in a more focused discussion on important elements of the deal structure. A key consideration was that Jafra's audited financials were incorporated into the Gillette company reports and had not been documented independently. This meant that for our financing, we needed an independent, stand-alone audited Jafra statement for each line item of expense and revenue that had been separated from the parent company. The 10-to-12-hour day ended with each team leaving for a brief dinner and an agreement to gather again that night.

Back in the conference room, each side was more animated and intransigent. It was late, people were tired, and patience was lagging. The morning's cordiality had evaporated, and several heated interruptions occurred. We ended at midnight and agreed to recommence in a few hours.

I caught the eye of Gillette's CFO, and he waited for me outside the conference room. We headed to a local bar to have a drink and discuss the sticking points. He shared with me their true bottom-line deal points, and I said I felt we could meet those revised expectancies. Just a few hours later, the CFO and I met again to confirm the central points we'd discussed and to make sure there were no misunderstandings after that long first day.

I then met with the CD&R partners and shared the insights I'd gained from talking to the Gillette CFO. We agreed that this provided a narrow window to secure an acceptable deal.

The second morning opened collegially. We offered revised terms that fit the general requirements the CFO had described to me. The Gillette team agreed. The deal was set to be announced to Jafra management in two days at the Four Seasons Biltmore Hotel in Santa Barbara, California.

Departing the Ropes law offices, I headed to the Boston airport for a brief flight to Newark, where my driver was waiting. He drove me home and waited while I picked up fresh clothes and another suit, and then he returned me to the airport to fly to Los Angeles for the announcement the next morning. Ron, Gonazalo, and I all wanted to be with the Jafra management team when the deal was released.

As I boarded the flight, a representative from the airline came to my seat and said I needed to call CD&R immediately. The deal had fallen apart, and the attorneys were meeting again in Boston. I called Steve Bachelder, my former law partner. Steve had relocated to Portland, Maine, less than two hours from Boston. Following a rapid debrief on the outstanding issues that had arisen, Steve drove to Boston to appear on my behalf. All my efforts were focused on pulling the deal back together.

Even in 1998, many aircraft had phones at the seats, though they were exorbitantly expensive to use. As we were taxiing for takeoff, I slid in my Amex card and called the Ropes and Gray conference room and was put on the speakerphone. Each side was calling foul on the other with abundant colorful language. I stayed on the line for the entire five-and-a-half-hour flight, seeking to find middle ground between the sides. I ended the call from the plane when we parked at the jet bridge in Los Angeles, but when I got off the plane, I reconnected from my cell phone. (I discovered a month later that my call from the plane cost nearly ten times the first-class ticket.)

The negotiations continued as I checked into my room at the Biltmore, ultimately concluding successfully at 7:00 a.m., just two hours before the announcement was scheduled. Crises averted. I took a coffee down to the beach to wake up. I had had little (or no) sleep over the last four days, but I could muse—job well done.

I was excited about this deal coming together because of a conversation I had had earlier with Ron. He, Gonzalo, and I had been traveling and visiting the Jafra operations in Europe, Mexico, and Latin America. I was serving as their lawyer and was focused on putting together the deal. In addition to ongoing transaction discussions with KKR and Jafra/Gillette management, Ron asked me to work with him on the business plan, mapping out Jafra's priorities and a forecast for the company post-acquisition. I had done this for other clients and enjoyed these non-traditionally legal aspects of operations and strategic planning.

Late one evening, on an overnight flight to London, while the bidding process was underway, Ron asked if I was interested in joining him to run the business. We agreed to discuss further if the deal was done. The evening of KKR's withdrawal, followed by the replacement of the funding by CD&R, cinched the deal. Ron and Gonzalo could not believe I had found a new financial partner—and $200 million—in less than18 hours. Frankly, I couldn't believe it myself.

The next morning, I told Ron, "I'm in. Let's get this deal closed and do something important together."

Knowing well that deals often fall apart for a variety of reasons, I deferred telling my law partners about my decision until the contracts were signed. When I did, they were incredulous.

"What do you know about cosmetics or direct sales," one of them asked.

"Nothing," I replied, "but I understand business strategy and executive talent. This company will have both."

Ron assembled a premier international team of network marketing professionals. All of them started their careers with his guidance during his 30-year tenure at Avon, when he was president of Avon USA as well as Avon Latin America. On the team was Eugenio Lopez Barrios, who started as a stock boy at Avon and rose through the ranks to become the president of Avon Mexico. Under Eugenio's leadership, Avon became the #1 direct seller in Mexico. When Ron departed for Mary Kay, Eugenio joined him as president of the Mary Kay Mexico, and in less than two years the company surpassed Avon as the top direct seller.

Eugenio became president of Jafra Mexico, our largest market globally. Jafra had more than 150,000 consultants in Mexico, and he was admired by all of them for his kindness and respect. He knew the first name of every one of his staff and greeted them all daily with a handshake or an embrace. He was a gifted natural leader, and even though I did not speak Spanish and Eugenio did not speak English, we became close friends.

In May 1998, the day following the closing of the transaction, the management team selected by Ron resigned their positions at Mary Kay, Avon, and several other companies to join Jafra. I was the only senior executive without operational or cosmetics experience, but Ron had great confidence in me as I left my law practice in New York and New Jersey to join Ron and Gonzalo as partners and together form the office of the chairman, where we would have responsibility for the global business. Ron was chairman, I was vice chairman, and Gonzalo was president. On the day of closing, we fired twenty-one executives, all of whom had jobs waiting for them at Gillette. We replaced them with six executives, including myself. John Rochon, the CEO of Mary Kay, was furious. On the day after the closing, he called Brian Finn, who asked me to be on the call with John and their attorneys. The call started uncomfortably and deteriorated quickly because John was angry. I listened passively for five or ten minutes.

As a quiet descended following his rant, John asked, "Rip, do you intend to take all of my executives?"

My response "No, John, only the good ones."

He was livid, and an already-bad call ended abruptly.

An interesting side note to this story is that 15 years later, John and his son John Jr. and I became good friends when he submitted a bid to buy LegalShield.

The main offices of Jafra Cosmetics were in California, so Ellen and I took the kids out of school, and we moved 3,000 miles to Montecito, where they did not know anyone. Taylor and Charlotte had just started school; Chris was a junior in high school and Stevie was a freshman. They attended the same school in Santa Barbara and were both selected for the varsity lacrosse team and played together like the iconic duo of Rich and Ron Sutter.

Before we left New Jersey, while Chris was in junior high, he was continuing to play elite hockey teams in New Jersey, New York, and Pennsylvania, and as he entered high school, top prep teams were in his pursuits, hoping to recruit him. It was a rigorous endeavor for both Chris and me as we had a practice several nights a week, and he played more than 80 games a season, including high school contests. Even while my corporate legal practice was flourishing, and I was traveling regularly to London, Prague and other places, I always kept an eye on Chris's practice and game schedules. Once a client sent me to Moscow, and in the midst of negotiations, I alerted the Russian bankers and lawyers that I had to leave right away to get to the airport. They were dumbfounded, and it felt like I had wheels in my feet. I was always on the move, never sitting still.

I do not recall if that one was an important practice, but all practices were important for me, so the rush was justified. With adrenaline coursing and everything timed to a dot, I arrived at the Sheremetyevo airport just a moment before the flight departed.

Eleven hours later, I landed at JFK. My driver had my hockey bag in the back seat, and I changed into my coaching gear and reached the rink moments before the practice began. I do not remember much other than shouts, sweat, and maybe an outline of strategy. What I do remember is getting under soft covers and sleeping in my bed that night.

Stevie was progressing well in hockey, but his real love was lacrosse. It made sense; not all kids share the same passion, and even if he and Chris were both naturals at sports, they had their preferences.

Shortly after the purchase of Jafra, we discovered that the business profits were one-third less than the financial restatement prepared by our accountants. As a former prosecutor, I was suspicious, and I began investigating. I queried our IT staff, and discovered that when Jafra was separated from Gillette, a number of shared services, including IT, ended the day of closing and all preclosing Jafra emails were removed.

I learned that backup tapes were available and arranged for the IT staff to perform a keyword search of them, looking for internal communications on earnings ("EBITDA"), "release of reserves," and "reversal." A host of emails dropped out between the Gillette's financial department and Jafra's CFO. We learned that reserve accounts had been released, which pumped up the stated earnings and inflated Jafra's operational results by one-third. The reserve release was not inappropriate, but two accounting firms had missed it. The resulting profits were positively affected by the release that was not based on the profitability of the current operations.

I assembled a comprehensive report, including the email evidence, which I was instructed to lose. We now owned this problem. Ron, Gonzalo, and I were facing a calamity and potential violations of our borrowing covenants. I set to work authoring an emergency plan, which I called "Project Lemonade"—as in, "If life gives you lemons, make lemonade." This aggressive plan had several key components, including the shutdown of our manufacturing plant in California and movement of all manufacturing to Mexico, where costs were 90 percent less. We also sold real estate adjacent to the offices and plants, and in Munich, we consolidated the support operations for our European companies and reduced redundant staff in Italy, Holland, Austria, and Switzerland.

The board enthusiastically approved Project Lemonade, and the timing was immediate. There was no going back. Jafra had to succeed. I had sold the home I loved in New Jersey and left behind its wonderful family history. I had also sold my interest in the law firm my partners and I founded. I was 3,000 miles from friends and much of my family. My kids were in new schools and separated from their friends in New Jersey. I had burned the boats. I did not sleep more than a few hours a night for nearly six months.

In less than ten days, I authored "Lemonade" by handwriting the text on yellow legal pads and handing the pages off to my talented assistant Lee Hidley. Lee was a former English teacher from New York. We hit it off immediately with abundant humor and dedication to excellence. For more than a week, I was at the office until midnight or later, leaving handwritten pages on Lee's desk. Each night as I left, the large offices, manufacturing plant, distribution facilities, and warehouse were empty. Only the night security guard was there, and he knew my name.

The coordination required to execute Lemonade was massive. Jamie Lopez Girao, our COO, was on our executive team, and he was an operational genius. He was head of operations at Avon for decades, and when he told them he was leaving to go to Jafra, they offered him a $5 million stay bonus. He declined and asked CEO Jim Preston why Avon had not properly recognized and rewarded his abilities during his time there. Jamie is a Spaniard and he was number 1 in his undergraduate and graduate engineering classes.

He was short, angered easily, and demanded excellence from the manufacturing and product distribution teams in the United States and Mexico. He was absolutely determined to make Jafra the best manufacturing operation globally. I always believed that part of his mission was to embarrass Avon.

Jamie gathered a handful of trusted lieutenants and rapidly put together a detailed plan to close the plant in Westlake Village, California, transferring most of the manufacturing to our Mexico facility. The remaining production work would be relocated on the day of the factory closing to a third-party operation in Chino, California. The mechanics had significant work to do before the equipment arrived later that day, and adjustments could be made to infrastructure, electrical connections completed, and water and sanitary-removal systems installed. They then waited to intercept the enormous transport trucks to unload and install the equipment removed from the factory. Their planning had to be accomplished in absolute secrecy. We met daily to review plans and timetables, which were loaded onto a schedule with every activity calendared down to the minute. The plan called for mechanics to arrive at the plant within minutes of the employees being notified that the factory was closing. The factory operations were massive. All of Jafra's skin-care and bodycare SKUs were manufactured and packaged there for shipment globally. The factory was FDA approved and certified as a pharmaceutical-grade facility. The employees wore sanitary outerwear and masks. There were enormous stainless steel mixing vats, some the size of a school bus.

Movers were scheduled to load the equipment remaining in California for transport to the third-party facility. The mechanics rode ahead of the trucks to spend the night rebuilding and reassembling the equipment to start production the next morning. Unbelievably, not one day of manufacturing was lost because this complex and detailed plan was put together so carefully.

We closed the factory that morning. The human resources team arrived early at my office, and the plan was for the head of HR to head down to the factory floor and make the announcement. Several hundred workers were there, and among them were fathers working with sons and nephews, second generations from the same families. "No," I told the HR team, "I will make the announcement myself. I authored Lemonade. It is my responsibility to face the staff." In an abundance of caution, I parked my car a half-mile away on a residential street.

We arranged a job fair at a conference facility across the street from the plant. At least 30 companies looking for trained workers were waiting for them. I made the announcement, and there were tears but also compassion. I thanked these workers for the excellence and dedication that had made Jafra the envy of cosmetics manufacturing. I told them about the job fair, and we gave each worker an envelope with $2,000 in cash. Their salaries and health insurance coverage also continued for two months. I was a bit shaken as several workers came up to me, offering tearful hugs and handshakes.

Within 24 hours, every worker had been offered a new job with wages at or above their Jafra salaries. Many of them had been traveling up to two hours each way, and their new jobs were close to home. I received a number of wonderful letters of thanks from them.

This was a lesson learned. There is no substitute for detailed planning. There is no substitute for bold, swift, and decisive action. This was a lesson I carried with me throughout my tenure operating six private equity businesses. Success is predicated on being nimble and dynamic and having the best team to execute plans. It is not a place for complacency or lack of confidence. Urgency is required.

Shortly after Lemonade was initiated, I was sitting in my office with a pile of papers on my desk. Ron had become my mentor and friend. He walked in, noting the stack of paperwork, and asked, "What are you doing here? This company will not grow if you are in the office. I can hire people to do that. You need to be out in the field. That is where the company will grow."

Taking Ron's advice, I was on the road weekly—to London, Munich (monthly), Mexico City (monthly), Vienna, Rome, São Paulo, Zurich, Moscow, and a host of other cities—to engage with the field leaders in each country, hosting dinners and conferences and speaking at their local meetings. I also led the company's regular communication with the partners at CD&R, where David Novak, Jesse Watson, and I became close friends and confidants. This schedule was demanding and challenging for a home life with young children.

I was invited each year to participate in the annual sales force meetings in several countries, including Germany and Italy. These multiple-day gatherings were much anticipated by the local field leaders and their recruits, which were known as their "down line." Each national meeting concluded with a formal banquet, and the Jafra "Ladies," as they were known, were out to impress with their beautiful gowns and immaculate hair and makeup.

I had taken German in high school and also a few years in college, and I was determined to offer my closing address in that language. A member of that country's executive team who was fluent in English worked closely with me on my pronunciation. As I walked out and started to speak in German at my first annual address, everyone jumped on their feet! In 45 years, no one from the Jafra world headquarters had ever addressed them in their language. They continued clapping and cheering as I fumbled my way through the remarks. My mispronunciations were forgiven, and the outpouring of enthusiasm was amazing. Each year this address became a source of pride for them, and I was honored to meet many of their families.

At Jafra, like other network businesses, advancement to the highest field positions was a source of pride. Top leaders received commissions for the sales that were secured by other field representatives they recruited. Successful top leaders made up to $1 million annually. At Jafra, the highest field position was Lady Grand Master. Germany had approximately 50 of these high achievers, Mexico had more than 150, and the United States had approximately 100. The Lady Grand Masters in each country wore to the final banquets a scarlet dress of a precise shade of red, though it was unique in the woman's own design. The bond these amazing leaders form with their down line was like family. They coached and assisted their new recruits, but they also shared a deep personal relationship, often celebrating holidays, birthdays, and vacations together with their teams.

The final moment of each country's banquet was the playing of the classic 1986 ballad "The Lady in Red," sung by British songwriter Chris de Burgh. As the song began, each Lady Grand Master stood at her table. Risers were placed at the front of the ballroom. Each Lady, starting with the most recently qualified, slowly walked to the risers. As the song concluded, the most senior Lady took her place. The assembled crowd, including myself, was in tears. It was exceptionally moving.

I witnessed this ceremony in other countries, and each time I was profoundly affected. These inspirational women saw this as more than a job. It was a calling. In many countries, particularly in Mexico and Latin America, these leaders have touched thousands through the coaching, sharing, and training of their recruits. Many of them were able to purchase their first home or to send the first member of their family to attend college.

On some nights, I was a bit overwhelmed by these women's confidence and by knowing I was responsible for protecting, preserving, and helping to grow their businesses. I had been afforded a unique opportunity to do something meaningful that had an impact on hundreds of thousands of these women's family members. As a lawyer, my decisions often had an impact on a company or on a limited group of individuals. This was very different. I was starting to understand what Ron, Gonzalo, and Eugenio have known for decades. This was more than a job—it was a mission-based calling.

Still today, if I hear "The Lady in Red," I am stirred with deep emotion and admiration.

In 1999, the Jafra USA national meeting was held at the Las Vegas Convention Center, and we took every room at the Paris Las Vegas Hotel. The hotel staff wore Jafra shirts, and Jafra pennants flooded the lobby. A few months before the meeting, our copresidents of Jafra USA, Bea Gutai and Diane Lucero, came to my office and asked if I would host the opening cocktail reception in the "big room" at Caesars Palace.

"You are asking a former trial attorney if he'd like to host a cocktail party for 5,000 people?" I said to them. "That is the dream of a lifetime!"

As they were leaving my office, they asked, "Is there anything special you would like?"

"Hey, it is Vegas," I responded. "Something with Siegfried and Roy would be good."

We all laughed as they departed.

On the day of the opening reception, Ron and I drove to Vegas together. He recommended that we not stay in the same hotel as the field and we were at the Venetian Hotel, which is near the Paris. I had several hours until the reception began across the street at Caesars and was settling into my room when I heard a knock on my door.

I opened the door, and there was an enormous security guard who said he had come to collect me for rehearsal. "Rehearsal for a cocktail party?" I asked. "I have been doing that since I was 18 years old."

Not to be denied, he escorted me to a private entrance at Caesars and the front doors of the theater. I opened the doors and saw two men and a cage at the end of the enormous room. They waved me toward them and said they were trainers who worked for Siegfried and Roy.

They were no taller than 5' 5" and each weighed perhaps 140 pounds. They were thin and wiry and in great shape. I was 6' and weighed 185 pounds. They asked me to sign two releases. One said I would never disclose the trick they were going to teach me. The other document was a full release for injury or death. I pointed out that if they ended up needing the second release, it didn't matter if they had the first one.

They laughed and began teaching me the escape trick. I would enter the cage, and then they would close the curtains, spin the cage once, and pull back the curtains to reveal that I had been replaced by an enormous Bengal tiger. I watched them carefully as they patiently tried to teach me the moves and technique, but I couldn't get it because I was simply too tall to contort myself and fit in the confined space of the escape route. We were running out of time, and I was sweating profusely from the exertion and attempts.

The trainers moved on to plan B, which would work because now I was able to exit the cage. I looked at my watch and told them I needed to leave immediately to get ready for the reception. Before I left, I completed the trick once, and one of the trainers said, "It took you fourteen seconds to complete the trick. You have eight seconds to get out. Once the trick starts, the cat will be in the cage in eight seconds, and we cannot stop it." They never showed me the cat.

When it came time for the trick, Diane and Bea lured me into the cage while 5,000 Jafra consultants, all having enjoyed unlimited drinks, cheered me on. I could smell the tiger, and the cage was shaking. I had no trouble this time exiting the cage in four seconds, well before the tiger entered. I appeared in the back of the room as the consultants cheered even more. What fun! I was scheduled to speak at the convention the next morning and walked onto the enormous stage to the pounding opening of the 1982 rock song "Eye of the Tiger" by Survivor. A tiger tail was hanging from the back of my suit. The crowd was on their feet, and that song became my walk-on introduction for the next six years at Jafra.

At the Jafra Italy meetings each summer, the awards presentations were among the highlights at the closing night banquet. Fabio Stillitano, a former Avon country manager and recent addition to the Jafra team as president of Jafra Italy, was a natural leader. He was charming and witty, and he was loved by the Italian field representatives.

Much like at the meetings in other countries, the ladies arrived resplendent in their best gowns and ready for a fun evening. The final award each year was presented to the associate who had sold the most products that year. At my third meeting, I noted that the same woman had won for several years. She was nicely dressed, like everyone else, but she was more conservatively attired and appeared a bit uncomfortable as she approached the stage.

"I'm a bit confused," I asked Fabio. "The same woman wins every year but does not appear very confident and seems shy."

Fabio laughed, and in his heavy Italian accent said, "Rip, I've been waiting for you to ask. She works in the home of Senor Gucci. Once a year, he places an enormous order with her, and at Christmas he gives Jafra cosmetics to all Gucci staff. He does it to help her earn some money and also so she gets recognized as the top seller. He loves her and her family."

In 2000, a highlight of attending these events occurred when I was invited to present at the World Federation of Direct Selling Associations meetings in Maui. Former president George H. W. Bush was the keynote speaker, and ten of us were invited to a private reception with him. He was affable, and we swapped stories about Ken Taylor while enjoying vodka on the rocks together.

I could not help but feel the surge of pride radiate from every sinew of my body as I saw Chris and Stevie, my two champions, side by side in action on the lacrosse field. They were destroying school after school in the league, and I was standing on the sidelines drenched in my emotions both as a father and a coach.

They each had different capabilities that shined the brightest individually without undermining the other. Chris, a terrific shooter, was also the team's "enforcer," frequently laying out unsuspecting players. He was a triple threat: strong, big, and someone who loved hitting. No one could move past his hulking physique because he was built for the field from an early age. If Chris was strength, Stevie was brains and agility. He was terrific at setting up scoring plays and ball handling. Whenever they were in the field, time slowed down, and everything played out in front of my eyes in 4k vision. It was magical and extraordinary.

I am not one to brag, but Chris was our golden boy. He was an outstanding student and an exceptional athlete. He was 6'2, handsome, and in great shape. Girls hovered around him like bees, and his charisma made them stick indefinitely. Everything was perfect. Ellen and I never thought that things could ever go haywire. The notion of change had been drilled into my head from an early age, so I was always aware of it, but that did not prepare me for the tidal change our family went through in late 2000 and early 2001.

Chris's behavior started to change, and he became distant and did not care for his years-old routines. His grades began to decline, and old friends were replaced by new ones I did not trust. He had his driving license and was on the brink of independence, and I refrained from making him feel small. One morning I got in the car to head to the gym and found a bag of grass in the back seat. It was a reality check because it told me how far Chris had gone in his teenage crisis; something my father would never have allowed me to go through.

What started as Chris's troubling behavior soon devoured the whole of our family. We were always on edge, ready to snap at one another if anyone spoke too soon or too loudly. The kids were tiptoeing around Ellen and me as we struggled to cope with the unforeseen situation. Chris's behavioral decline was rapid and draining. It broke us and leeched the joy from our household. Taylor and Charlotte were in grammar school and were still unaware of the things that were troubling the adults of the household.

Chris began disappearing for days at a time, and I drove around Santa Barbara, tracking his trail many nights. I returned home in the morning, took a quick shower, and went to work. It was an exhausting time and was unlike anything we had ever faced. I was determined that we could pull through it.

My efforts did not pay off, and the fabric of our family started unraveling right before our eyes. Ellen and I were always at odds with each other, and the unrest that Chris's troubling behavior triggered was never resolved. There was a crack in our relationship, and I realized it was impossible to make everything whole again. My 50th birthday was on August 21, 2001, and we had arranged a multiple-day birthday celebration. Friends arrived from New York, Europe, Latin America, and Canada. Ken and Pat Taylor came to stay at our home.

A few weeks later, I was in New York on September 9 and 10 to negotiate a refinancing for Jafra at the Merrill Lynch offices next to the World Trade Center. I had visited these offices often during in my corporate legal career. I represented William Schreyer, the CEO and chairman of Merrill Lynch. My usual journey was to take a train to Newark's Penn Station and from there take the Path train to the stop under the World Trade Center towers. I got out there and took a land bridge across the street to Merrill Lynch. For this trip, I was scheduled to return to Los Angeles on September 11, but we concluded the Jafra negotiations on the 10th, and I elected to catch the last flight out of JFK back to California that evening.

Early on the morning of 9/11, following a short night with little sleep, I was at the Montecito gym for my daily workout. I was alone there on the cross trainer, breathing hard and working up a sweat, when shortly after 5:46 a.m. PDT (8:46 in New York), the CNN broadcast was interrupted to report that a plane had hit the North Tower at the World Trade Center. I was confused. The weather in

New York was perfect when I departed just a few hours earlier. I have a pilot's license, although it has been years since I had piloted a plane.

They cut to the scene at the Trade Center, where smoke was billowing from the North Tower, painting the brilliant blue sky in gray and black. In close-ups, I saw people above the impact point waving handkerchiefs out open windows. As I watched the live feed, another large airliner appeared and flew into the South Tower at 6:03 a.m. PDT. I recall shouting, "No!" at the screen. Leaping from the cross trainer, I exclaimed, "We are under attack!"

Dread pooled in my gut as I knew from my years working in lower Manhattan that thousands of people would already be in the towers. I left the gym, and my phone started ringing as I jumped in the car. It was my brother Tom. "Aren't you flying back from NY today?" he asked, worry evident in his voice.

After putting his concerns to rest, I raced back home to Ellen and the kids. I woke them and told them what had happened as we sat in front of the television. We stared open-mouthed as the first tower collapsed and chaos ensued. We found ourselves offering prayers.

Several hours later, my phone rang again. It was Chris Johnson, the head of credit at Merrill Lynch. He had just landed at LAX on a flight from New York. We were scheduled to meet the next day at the Jafra offices. He was calling me from the Hertz rental car counter.

"Rip, I just landed," he said. "All the flights have been grounded. I have the last car in the Hertz inventory. I am driving back to New York, so my family is not alone."

The September 11 attacks were shocking, and I am glad we were able to be together as a family that day, but it was already a difficult time for us. Ellen and I were getting divorced one month later. The years have healed the wounds, and even now, Ellen and I are cordial with each other. We correspond about our kids and bond over the blessing of their happiness.

Ellen and I were separated for a year or so before the divorce, and I took up residence with Ron Clark in Ojai, a beautiful and small

California town just south of Montecito. Ron's house was a menagerie with his dog Frankie, his bird Maia, and tropical fish. The air was filled with the sound of some activity from either the dog or the bird. It was never silent. His older son, Logan, was also staying with us, making the house a home to three bachelors and nothing short of a frat house.

The house was built in the early 1920s and was once the home of Hollywood actress Loretta Young. It was also a getaway for Richard Nixon, who loved the golf course there. We lived on the grounds of the Ojai Country Club, the site of many PGA Tour events. It was a world of luxury as the club delivered meals to the door.

All the fun aside, something peculiar occurred when I was living there that was also quite spooky. My room was next to the kitchen, and on one of my first few nights sleeping in the house, I woke up to the sound of activity outside my door. The next morning at the office, Ron inquired, "How did you sleep?" I told him about the noise from the kitchen and suggested that Frankie should stay in my room so he wouldn't be in the kitchen.

"Frankie was in my room all night," Ron responded. Seeing the perplexed look on my face, he further clarified, "He spends his nights with me."

Now my bewilderment was reaching new heights because I knew what I had heard.

Finally, Ron declared, "Rip, the house is haunted."

We laughed at the possibility of a ghost in the house, and he shared with me numerous paranormal episodes he had experienced over the years. In one incident, he returned home from the Jafra offices to find his contractor and helpers in their van. They said they had seen a spirit drift through the room where they were working. They were all the grown men, and they were shivering from having just seen a shadow pass through the room. Hilarious and spooky at the same time.

I am a skeptic, so it takes a lot more than just accounts of ghost tales and a few noises to convince me that any kind of supernatural antics have occurred. Throughout my stay there, I woke up to other unusual sounds and noises coming from the kitchen. Sometimes, I found drawers and even a refrigerator opened the next morning. I should have felt dread or fear, but I became accustomed to the disruptions that ensued most nights. It became so common that whenever I woke up to these noises, I shouted, "Hey! Cut it out. I have to work in the morning." The noises always stopped after my outbursts, like a switch being flipped.

New Year's Eve in 2002 was a turning point. The divorce from Ellen was concluded, and I was ready to start a new life in Beverly Hills. That night, I attended a gathering at Mr. Chow's. I was sitting at a large table with seven seats. Tony and Ridley Scott, both wearing baseball caps, walked in with their wives. As they entered, flashes of camera lights went off, and paparazzi toppled over one another to secure the best photo. Ridley's film *Gladiator* had won the 2001 Academy Award for Best Picture, Best Actor, and five other categories. Ridley's wife, the Brazilian actress Giannina Facio, had played Russell Crowe's wife in *Gladiator*. Donna Scott, Tony's wife, was a Fembot (gynoid) in *Austin Powers* and played Tom Cruise's girlfriend in *Days of Thunder*. Both couples were stealing the spotlight at the time. Al Pacino was sitting beside me at the table. It was a crazy night!

I remember dancing and drinking with the Scott brothers and their wives until early in the morning. They were charming, very relaxed, and did not act like Hollywood snobs. Our conversation was filled with lots of laughter as everyone enjoyed a pleasant night. Several times during the evening, I asked them about their incredible movies and success, but they only wanted to talk about Jafra.

"What's it like to run a real company? We have never met anyone who's done that," they commented.

In Beverly Hills, I was residing in a small gated community on Benedict Canyon near Mulholland Drive. My neighbors included Bob Shapiro, who defended O. J. Simpson, as well as Seal and his wife Heidi Klum. It was a short drive to LAX, and considering that I was continuing to travel often to support the 16 Jafra operations in Europe, Latin America, and Mexico, it was convenient and efficient. The Beverly Hills Hotel was just down the road and served as my clubhouse. A typical day consisted of business meetings, drinks, and dinners after work. I started to date and met some fascinating women around that time, but I was not ready to move into a permanent relationship. It felt too early to commit to another woman when I was still coping with my divorce. Time passed by as I indulged in casual relationships, mindless flirtations, and friendly dates. Work obligations hindered my schedules and opportunities.

Mom and Dad Sanibel Island, FL. Circa 1980

Rip The Long Trail, VT. 1981-1985

Tom Mason, Rip and Dave Sheldon The Long Trail, VT. 1981-1985

Sailing on the Chesapeake with Dad Chesapeake. 1986

Taylor and Charlotte Harbourton, NJ. 1993

Taylor and Charlotte Harbourton, NJ. 1995

Charlotte – Princeton, NJ. 1995

Taylor and Charlotte Easter Sunday. 1995

Skylink Operations Baghdad, Irag. 2006

Rip and Diana Vermont. 2016

Colin, Kennedy, Taylor and Charlotte Goshen, VT. 2018

Charlotte, Colin and Taylor - The Waterside Inn, Bray-Maidenhead, UK. 2019

Taylor, Charlotte and I Paris. 2019

Taylor and I Pennington, NJ. 2019

Charlotte and Taylor New York. 2023.

Kennedy Goshen, VT. 2020

(L to R) College roommate Charles Cavness, cousin Jeff Marcks and I Middlebury College Snow Bowl. 2021

Diana and I Christmas morning, Goshen, VT. 2021

Lady Slipper Lane Goshen, VT. 2022

Carpe Diem 70th birthday (L to R) my sister Karen, Colin, Jill, Taylor, Charlotte and Kennedy, Goshen, VT. 2021

Orient Express Paris to Venice. 2021

Chapter 7

Cradle Holdings, Skylink, Neways

Jafra continued to grow from 2000 to 2003. A perfect storm geared to terrific sales increases chiefly in Mexico, under the fatherly guidance of Eugenio, who was beloved by the consultants. Sales were also driven up globally by my great friend Alan Fearnley's massive repositioning of the product line. Alan is a Brit and came out of the Avon experience, where he successfully grew the Avon business in Germany while he was in his 20s.

The financial results at Jafra were also enhanced by the efforts of my friend and CFO Mike DiGregorio, the only senior Gillette executive we retained following our purchase. He was a driven CPA, having grown up in the Gillette financial offices. A graduate of Wharton, Mike was fluent in English and Spanish, and his wife Ari was Mexican. Mike and I worked closely on financial reports and briefings for CD&R, the board, our bankers, and the rating agencies (Moody's and Standard & Poor's). Mike contained expenses and kept challenging local markets on their budgets.

From 1999 to 2004, Jafra was the fastest-growing major network sales business in the world. Ron, Gonzalo, Mike, Alan, and I held quarterly meetings for the employees, and they cheered and celebrated when they learned about our comparative results and world-leading growth. It was a marvelous result of hard work, focus, and dedication. We were aligned in our firm belief that field consultants were the key to success. We honored their accomplishments and growth. The staff and field leaders had a spring in their step.

Work was hard. Long days, short nights—abundant hours spent on flights. But it was fun, and we were crushing it.

Jafra's USA operations were its original market when the company was founded in 1956 by Jan and Frank Day. The company name was a construct of the first few letters of their names (Ja Fra). In an interesting coincidence, Jan attended my alma mater Middlebury College where she graduated in 1946. My Middlebury connections would emerge again in later private equity operations during my career. Jan had also worked with Mary Kay Ash (the founder of Mary Kay Cosmetics) and Mary Kay's cousin Mary Crowley at Stanley Home Products. These pioneering women became friends at Stanley, and that's where they developed their love of direct sales. They believed passionately in creating independent business opportunities for women. Crowley went on to found Home Interiors and Gifts, Inc., another major direct-selling company.

We recognized that the Jafra USA business was comprised of two segments—one of English-speaking women and another supported by Spanish-speaking women—and we created two divisions of the American business. Each unit had its own president. I spoke at both annual conventions. In 2003, the Spanish division hosted several thousand independent consultants at their annual meeting in San Antonio, TX. I had a Jafra board meeting at our offices north of Los Angeles on the day the convention opened, and that evening Ron and I hosted a dinner for the board members. I had booked a private plane departing at midnight to take me to Texas for the next morning's opening.

I reached the hotel and a beautiful top-floor suite after 2:30 a.m. I was looking forward to a few hours of sleep as I entered the rooms and noticed that all the televisions were on, and I could hear a Spanish baritone as I started to unpack my bag. As I was taking out my suit for the morning, I glanced at the television and was floored to see myself on the screen. They had taken my address from the previous year and dubbed it into Spanish, and it was playing on a continuous loop throughout the hotel.

As I opened the convention the next morning, I recounted this story and the surprise I had found on my television. The consultants, all of whom were in on the ruse, were delighted. In closing, and evoking even more extended laughter, I noted that my Spanish was indeed excellent.

In Spring 2004, following six years of operations at Jafra, management and CD&R, our private equity sponsor, determined that it was time to sell the company and return profits to the investors and the management team. We commenced discussions on strategic alternatives.

Merrill Lynch arranged several meetings in Paris for me with executives at LVMH, the luxury consumer-goods company with premier brands, including Louis Vuitton, Dior, Givenchy, and other elite labels. I also met in New York with Ronald Lauder, the CEO of prestige brands, including Estée Lauder, Bobbi Brown, Clinique, and Aveda. LVMH and Lauder were both interested in Jafra. They loved our product line, packaging, and first-to-market strategy, where we introduced many new ingredients, including exotic botanicals from the Amazon. They ultimately determined not to pursue the company because we were a direct-to-consumer brand and all of their holdings were retail.

CD&R elected to file for an initial public offering (IPO), a decision I did not support. The company was relatively small, which would result in little retail stock investment and leave the stock price vulnerable to the whims of institutional investors. CD&R set up a number of meetings with Wall Street analysts, who would provide coverage for Jafra following the public stock offering. I worked with our legal team to draft an S-1 registration statement with the SEC, the first step in a public stock offering. We held all-night meetings at the law firm in New York. This was an exceptionally detailed and highly regulated document and process. Finally, the S-1 was completed and approved by the accountants, lawyers, bankers, and CD&R. It was then filed with the SEC under my signature.

Several days later, we were contacted by Vorwerk, a German family investment trust that owned several direct-sales brands in Europe. The S-1 facilitated their rapid understanding of the business and its financial performance. Within weeks, they made an offer above the suggested IPO pricing offered by our bankers, and we rapidly entered into an agreement. Diligence commenced with a host of Vorwerk executives and owners visiting the Jafra operations in the United States, Mexico, and Europe. I accompanied them on their visits and interviews.

In May 2004, Jafra was sold to Vorwerk, and the returns to CD&R were exceptional, significantly above the market. My management team and I emerged with tremendous financial success along with offers to continue running Jafra after the purchase. It became clear, however, that Vorwerk did not provide management equity incentives or options to anyone outside the family. During an interesting allteam meeting in Mexico City, I advised their CEO that as owners of a U.S.-based company now, offering equity for management was the norm for attracting and retaining top talent. He was polite and complimentary in his response, noting the opportunity for significant bonuses, including a bonus to stay on at Jafra.

I kept my counsel and resigned the day after the sale. I was 53 years old and was entering prime time for operating executives. I would dearly miss Ron, Gonzalo, Eugenio, Alan, and Mike, but it was time to move on. The phone started ringing as other companies began reaching out. As I explained to friends later, "When you sell a company with the investment returns like we secured at Jafra, people think you actually know something."

A number of attractive offers came in. I was pursued to take over the management of two independent prestige couture firms in Europe and several other direct and retail cosmetics businesses. I decided to accept an offer to run Cradle Holdings, owned by Fox

Paine, a private equity fund headquartered near San Francisco. Cradle was comprised of three prestige brands.

Dr. Erno Laszlo was the name behind the first cosmetics brand developed by an MD. Founded nearly 70 years earlier by Dr. Laszlo, it was utilized widely by Hollywood luminaries, including Brigitte Bardot, Marilyn Monroe, Audrey Hepburn, and more recently by Jackie Onassis, Madonna, and Nicole Kidman. The brand was exceptional, but it needed to be modernized and updated to appeal more broadly to a new and affluent generation that enjoyed many exceptional product choices. Laszlo was available only at prestige retail doors, including Saks, Bergdorf (where we had the only treatment spa in-store), Nieman, Nordstrom, and Barneys New York.

The second brand was Penhaligon's, which was founded more than 140 years earlier. This lovely British brand was renowned for its fragrances and exquisite gifts. Their signature fragrance, Blenheim Bouquet, had been formulated by Henry Penhaligon more than 100 years earlier. It was a personal favorite of Winston Churchill. We were told that it was frequently worn by Tom Ford, the top designer at Gucci. Penhaligon's enjoyed an extensive fragrance library, with standalone retail stores throughout London and in New York and on Rodeo Drive in Beverly Hills. We also had a standalone store in the Forum Shops at Caesars Palace in Las Vegas. Penhaligon's was a leading seller of fragrance counters in top retail stores, including Saks, Bergdorf, Nieman, Nordstrom, and Barneys New York.

Cradle Holding's third brand was L'Artisan Parfumeur. Located in Paris, L'Artisan was a jewel in the fragrance world. The brand hosted a broad array of fragrances, all developed by Pamela Roberts, the "nose" of the brand. The flagship store in Paris was next to the Louvre, and there a number of other standalone stores throughout the city and outside it.

The corporate offices in Place Vendôme in Paris were directly across the plaza from the Ritz and were formerly the residence of Frédéric Chopin. When I became CEO at Cradle, I was advised that my Paris office had once been Chopin's bedroom. In the United States. we were the leading fragrance at each of the major prestige doors, including Bergdorf, Barneys, and Saks. We built a standalone store in the tony area of SoHo downtown in New York.

When I arrived at the Laszlo offices in New York, I was surprised to learn that the operations team did not have the "product library formulations," the term for the ingredients, their proportions, and the processes for creating the product. Even though the libraries had been acquired several years previously, that information remained with the seller. I immediately had the team secure the library, but this revelation was both revealing and disturbing. Within a month, Laszlo was about to launch a new high-technology skin-care product designated as Transphuse, which would premiere at Bergdorf Goodman in New York. The company had purchased full-page ads with photography in the Bergdorf catalog. I began asking about the basic product testing for stability and consumer use and was stunned to discover that it had not been undertaken. I advised my financial partners at Fox Paine that I was canceling the launch.

The product development costs and advertising were a total loss, but without the fundamental testing, the launch was a risk I was unwilling to take for the company. I hired my close friend Alan Fearnley to take over as president of Laszlo, and we started to work immediately with Susan Goldsberry, a preeminent skin-care formulator from California, whom we had worked with previously.

Susan was a gifted developer with cutting-edge insights into skin care and new-ingredient opportunities. Over the course of three months, we formulated a replacement for Transphuse, incorporating a new first-time Amazon botanical and stressing the testing procedures to simulate multiple-year storage and product stability. We also undertook standard consumer-use tests to ensure that the formulation did not result in irritation or other unintended side effects. New packaging with the imagery of a test tube was designed for the product. Alan dubbed Transphuse a "cosmeceutical." Bergdorf, Saks, Neiman, and other prestige outlets were enthusiastic, and Transphuse became the biggest-selling product in Laszlo's 70-year history.

We were determined to reach a broader audience with the Laszlo line, and I started the production of a TV infomercial. Casting was critical. Dr. Frank Ryan, the renowned Beverly Hills plastic surgeon and my good friend, agreed to appear in the infomercial. Frank and I rode motorcycles together, and I visited his ranch in the mountains above Malibu, where he had a petting zoo for visiting intercity children. In addition to his exceptional practice, he offered free tattoo removal for gang members. Frank was a regular guest on television and appeared on Entertainment Tonight and other shows. We enjoyed each other's company and dined together frequently.

We next searched for a host for the Laszlo infomercial. I contacted Jack King, a notable celebrity-casting agent, and with his guidance interviewed three top candidates. Jack and I met at the Beverly Hills Hotel, my local watering hole and clubhouse, and I advised him that I did not believe any of the three were right for our infomercial.

Jack suggested that the best host who fit my description of the person I wanted was Emma Samms, the British actress best known for the hit TV show Dynasty. He did caution me that she had been asked before about hosting or being involved in other advertising efforts, and she had never agreed to do it in the past. He said he knew her agent, and at my request, he called him while we are having lunch. The agent responded that Emma was not interested in infomercials or product endorsements.

I asked Jack, who was still on the phone, to inquire where Emma was. The agent responded that she was in Bucharest, Romania, shooting a movie. I asked if she would meet me the next night in Bucharest for dinner, and I would describe the project in a face-to-face meeting. The agent laughed and could not believe I was serious. He reached out to Emma, who agreed to have a dinner meeting with a crazy CEO based in Los Angeles, one who would fly overnight to meet her.

I went directly to LAX and boarded a flight to Frankfurt and changed planes there and arrived the next day in Bucharest. Emma and I met for dinner, swapped stories, and enjoyed a wonderful conversation assisted by two bottles of Bordeaux. At the end of the evening, Emma agreed to host the Laszlo infomercial, which would be filmed on an LA sound stage the next week. Emma's husband was American, and we all became great friends and often met in London for lunch or dinner.

Each of the Cradle Holdings brands had an independent office. Laszlo operations in New York were on Fifth Avenue across from Bergdorf. Penhaligon's offices were in central London, off Piccadilly, while L'Artisan's headquarters were in Paris. I leased a lovely apartment in the Olympic Tower on 51st Street and Fifth Avenue in New York. Olympic Tower was developed by Aristotle Onassis. My apartment on the 31st floor had exceptional views. It looked north up Fifth Avenue across Central Park. I could see Yankee Stadium, the George Washington Bridge, and the Palisades. To the west, I looked down to Rockefeller center with a view of the Christmas tree and the *Today* show outdoor audience area.

I was living in Beverly Hills and arranged my travel schedule to depart Los Angeles for New York on Monday mornings. After five days in the Laszlo offices, I took an overnight flight to London, where I remained at the Halkin hotel, managed by my close friend Kuno Fasel. Kuno arranged for the concierge to hold my clothes, including suits, ties, and dress shirts, along with a shaving kit and toiletries. This allowed me to board the flights without luggage and quickly exit Heathrow upon arrival.

After several days at Penhaligon's offices, I headed to Waterloo station and boarded the Eurostar to Paris for meetings at L'Artisan. I stayed at Hotel de Crillon on the Place de la Concorde, and the staff was incredibly accommodating and held my suits, clothing, and other items for me. If you have to travel for business, I am convinced that you cannot do it better.

I returned on an overnight flight to Los Angeles every other weekend to see my kids for visitation. After the weekend, I left on Monday for New York to start the two-week cycle again.

At L'Artisan, Pamela Roberts had received an exciting inquiry from the producers of flowers used to develop perfume oils. The flower growers typically blended the pedals from a variety of fields for processing and extraction of the oils. Our largest flower producer in France noted that not all growing geographies produced the same concentration of oils. Annually, specific fields produce superior and exceptional high-oil content flowers, and certain flowers grow better depending on the soil and weather conditions each year. Rather than blending these petals with ones from a less superior harvest, he said he could reserve the exceptional varietals for the L'Artisan production of a unique and unrivaled fragrance.

These discussions launched what became known as Grand Cru. The finest flowers, from the best fields, produced that year would be processed for a special limited edition L'Artisan fragrance. Our marketing department created a beautiful crystal decanter, each one numbered and presented in a wooden box reminiscent of Bordeaux wine packaging. Hence the designation Grand Cru.

There was incredible excitement at L'Artisan as we prepared for the release of the first Grand Cru fragrance. In New York, I met with the CEOs of Saks, Bergdorf, and Barneys New York, where we already enjoyed top sales status. A fascinating bidding war ensued, with each of these prestigious doors vying for exclusivity. I advised store management that any exclusivity would be strictly limited to a one-month advantage over other stores and that our standalone doors would also offer Gran Cru at that same time.

Each of these elite retailers offered us the covers of their catalogs and premier placement at their flagship store entrances in New York. As the discussions progressed, I held a final meeting with the CEO at Barneys and told him we would grant Barneys a one-month exclusive if we received window placement at their flagship store on Madison Avenue. The CEO said he would absolutely make a full-window display available to us. I countered by observing, "I do not think you understand. I want all of the windows."

The CEO responded that Barneys had never given any single vendor access to all its windows. As I stood to exit the meeting, he laughed and responded, "You've got it. I want the exclusive."

Grand Cru was a complete sales success and sold out rapidly. We had a big celebration when I return to Paris.

In late 2005, I was called by Steve Bachelder. His executive compensation practice had grown tremendously, and he was highly regarded and widely sought out by corporate executives for his advice and counsel regarding the negotiation and design of their compensation packages.

Steve represented numerous business leader clients, and among them was the president of a division at Disney. The executive, whom I had met earlier, told Steve that Disney might consider a sale of ABC, the television network. The Walt Disney Company had acquired Capital Cities/ABC in 1995 in a $19 billion merger. At the time of the merger, ABC owned 80 percent of ESPN, the sports cable network. The media industry was undergoing a consolidation with Westinghouse putting together a $5 billion transaction to buy CBS.

Bob Iger was the chief operating officer of Cap Cities/ABC at the time of the merger, and in 2000, he was named the president of Disney and in 2005 the company's CEO. Turmoil erupted between cable providers and the major television networks. Cable was originally designed to serve rural areas that had little access to TV programming, but the business exploded when cable began offering exclusive channels such as CNN and HBO. Early on, cable providers could only offer approximately 36 channels and could easily fill their programming without local networks, including ABC, CBS, and NBC.

The Federal Communications Commission (FCC) created a "must carry" rule that required cable carriers to offer all local TV network broadcasts. The cable companies paid a fee to the major networks to carry their feed but had discretion in setting the rates for customers. This resulted in routine block outs of the networks as the fees were generally subject to renegotiation every three to five years.

Cable's growth put a squeeze on the television networks' revenues. Many networks chose to capitulate to the cable provider fee proposals in order to maintain their consumer connection and advertiser revenues. This fostered Disney's reasons for considering a sale of ABC.

I placed a call to Steve Waters as a first, respectable approach to Disney to assess their interest. I had been introduced to Steve in 2003, and during our first meeting, as he learned more about Jafra, he picked up the phone and called Ron Lauder, the CEO and chairman of Estée Lauder, the prestige cosmetics company. "Ron," he said, "I want you to meet Rip Mason and learn about Jafra. This is a company you should own."

Steve was the cofounder of the New York–based Compass Partners, and he was a Wall Street legend. From 1988 to 1996, Steve had been at Morgan Stanley, as the cohead of mergers and acquisitions.

After the call, I traveled to New York and met with Steve and several of his associates and walked them through my preliminary thoughts on the potential purchase of ABC from Disney. Steve loved the idea and agreed to work with me in framing a transaction memo to share with several major New York private equity firms. Private equity money strongly aligns with experienced management, and I would be in charge of sourcing the lead executives of ABC if we succeeded with the purchase.

One of my friends and fraternity brothers at Middlebury College was Terry McGuirk, who from 1996 to 2001 was the CEO of Turner Broadcasting, which owned CNN. I called Terry, and after we caught up about life and family, I asked if he would come in as CEO of ABC. Terry believed his broadcasting career was over and had recently been named chairman of the Atlanta Braves. He suggested I reach out to Jeff Sagansky, who had been president of CBS and had an exceptional media resume.

In moments, I was talking to Jeff and describing the potential transaction. Jeff chuckled and was supportive. I said we should also name a chief operating officer with deep industry expertise, and Jeff suggested that I call Didier Pietri, a former COO of ABC with extensive ABC network experience. I spoke to Didier that afternoon, and, like Jeff, he was supportive and agreed to be COO.

Jeff, Didier, and I gathered in New York with Steve Waters and his team. Jeff suggested that I come in as president of ABC when the deal closed. My primary assignment would be to negotiate a new cable carry arrangement to compensate the network properly for their content and viewer base. Jeff and Steve believed that my success in deal negotiations and absence of media experience and bias would be a plus in crafting a new paradigm in network compensation.

I worked with Steve to complete the transaction memo while he arranged a preliminary meeting with a major New York private equity fund. To approach Disney, we needed unequivocal access to the capital to complete a deal. Our preliminary valuation suggested that the transaction would be approximately $8 billion.

The initial meeting with the fund was a resounding success. They approved the use of their name in support of the transaction and encouraged us to reach out to Disney to assess their interest.

The transaction memo included extensive financial modeling and a detailed strategic plan outlining operational, marketing, and sales activities post-transaction. It took weeks to assemble, and at the same time, I continued my biweekly trips from home in Beverly Hills to San Francisco, attending Cradle board meetings, along with regular visits to New York, Paris, and London. It was exhausting but fascinating. I was also juggling time with the kids and attempting to sync up appointments and overseas travel with our times together. I ultimately departed Fox Paine to be engaged fully as member of a qualified buying group that was pursuing the Disney/ABC deal.

Steve Waters was friends with one of the most senior executives at Disney. Steve previewed our proposal to his friend and noted the experience of the management team we had assembled, and he pointed out the support of a world-renowned private equity partner with unquestionable resources to fund the transaction. The Disney executive responded favorably and offered to speak to his board and other senior executives. Some weeks went by, and he reached back to Steve. Disney was interested in the proposal, but the consensus was that the timing was not ideal to consider the sale.

The rejection of the approach was disappointing, but Disney's decision was not necessarily all bad news. The engagement of top-tier management and confirmation of multi-billion-dollar financing furthered my reputation as a dealmaker and executive manager. It was time to move on to new pursuits.

Laboring successfully in the cosmetics world, with postings at Jafra and the elite prestige brands of Erno Laszlo, Penhaligon's, and L'Artisan Parfumeur, put me on a fast track to continue with different cosmetics business opportunities. I was also courted to run several couture fashion brands in Europe. Instead, I entered a new and decidedly different chapter. Routine travel and meetings in Paris, Rome, New York, Milan, and London were replaced with the dust of the desert and the violence of the Middle East in a time of war.

Many people learn about the triumphs and turmoil of war through mainstream media. They shudder at the depiction of violence while reading Tolstoy's *War and Peace* and frown upon the horrors in Homer's *The Iliad* and *The Odyssey*. Hollywood has earned large sums by twisting the narrative in its war movies. War and military service were part of my family legacy for generations. The roots of it go back to Pappy's grandfather, my great-great-grandfather, John Harris. He fought at Chancellorsville and Gettysburg and other major battles in the Civil War. Witnessing Pappy's sorrow and my dad's hesitancy to divulge secrets, I came to appreciate how war broke men's spirits and played with their minds. Neither of them ever shared the gory details of their time in the service, but the new generation learned to connect dots as we grew old.

I had been introduced to the founders of Skylink by my friend Ken Taylor, who was a member of the company's board of directors and knew the Toronto-based company well through his years-long association. Skylink was a business that provided planes and helicopter services to the United Nations, the Canadian government, and, on occasion, to the USAID—an entity managed by the US Department of State. On the surface, everything looked exciting and revolutionary, but the reality was far from it. Skylink's services were provided in the most dangerous areas of the world, often in times of war, and included the transportation of food, medical supplies, and personnel. Their equipment, including helicopters and jet aircraft, was provided primarily out of Eastern Europe, where, following the fall of the Soviet Union, much of the military needs had ended. The pilots and flight crews were predominantly former Russian military officers.

Their contracts were typically for a limited duration and were often extended as conflicts continued.

In May 2006, I was asked to negotiate a Letter of Intent to purchase Skylink. Immediately following, I worked with their president Jan Ottens to arrange diligence trips to their primary areas of operations in Baghdad, Iraq, and Darfur, in Sudan. World history bears witness that both sites were not places to be at the time because of the violence and death happening there. They were active war zones stained with blood. The Skylink founders suggested I meet with their local executives in Dubai, but I declined. I wanted to see the operations on the ground and meet unrestrained with their field personnel. One would think that technological advancement and the global village would make nations put the violence of the 20th century behind them. Instead, 9/11 got the 21st century off to a horrendous start, and it accelerated in March 2003 when the US-led coalition invaded Iraq, following months of UN and US government charges of "noncompliance" with the first Iraq war's cease-fire requirements. As the United States became an occupying force in Iraq, several insurgent groups emerged, including one founded by

Abu Musab al-Zarqawi. His offshoot of al-Qaeda in Iraq ultimately became ISIS.

An ethnic conflict between Sunni and Shia Muslims led to atrocities on both sides. Al-Qaeda in Iraq attacked both US personnel and Shia Muslims, often beheading any adversaries. Zarqawi's brutality was so extreme that ultimately, he lost al-Qaeda's support. The United States posted a reward for his capture equal to the bounty offered for Osama Bin Laden.

My diligence trip started in June 2006 with an overnight flight to Dubai, where I prepared for the Skylink services flight to Baghdad. Flying at approximately 30,000 feet from Dubai and directly over the Baghdad airport, the 727's pilot announced that he was commencing a vertical descent. He banked the plane tightly to the right with its nose pointed directly to the ground. The sound of acceleration was deafening. I was surrounded on the plane by Halliburton roughnecks who were working on Iraq oil fields and by several US Marines.

As the plane gained velocity, there was a feeling of total absence of control. Several passengers were vomiting while others were screaming. A corkscrew landing was designed to provide maximum protection from missile attack and was accomplished in a tight cylindrical pattern directly above the airport. I was delighted that I did not scream or vomit, but it was indeed a moment of terror in the sky. That feeling continued on the ground as insurgent operations sponsored by Abu Musab al-Zarqawi and others had managed to terrorize the whole city.

Skylink was engaged in a host of services for the US and other coalition forces, including operating the civilian flights in and out of the Saddam International Airport that provided food, medicine, personnel, flight refueling, and transportation for approximately 100,000 Halliburton civilian employees. The Halliburton staff served in theater in Iraq for three weeks and then rotated out to Dubai for a week. Skylink also provided logistics and ran crop-dusting missions.

When I landed in Baghdad, I was collected by Skylink operational executives and led to the immigration counter, where I was issued a visa in real-time. The visa required a reason for the trip, and it was noted as "Emergency." After concluding my meetings and facilities tour in Baghdad, I returned to the airport, headed to Dubai, and upon takeoff from Iraq we repeated the cylindrical ascent. Nearly 20 minutes into the flight, the plane leveled off at 30,000 feet directly over the airport.

In Dubai, I had arranged a dinner for the Skylink Baghdad staff at a restaurant on the top floor of the Emirates Tower hotel. It was a gorgeous private room, well-appointed with the finest liquors, wines, and Cuban cigars. Most of the Skylink team were former SAS, Royal Marine, and special forces personnel from the United Kingdom and Australia. It was a sensational dinner filled with toasts and swapping of stories. Everyone was relaxed and enjoyed the evening, a juxtaposition to the violence in Baghdad just a few hours away.

When it was time to order the wine for dinner, an attractive Russian waitress offered me a tasting for approval. As she leaned in to pour, I noted a distinctive fragrance. "Are you wearing attar of roses?" I asked, then continued, "that smells like Joy, and it is perfect on you." She stood back, open-mouthed and shocked at my observation. "That is exactly what I am wearing. How did you know?" I smiled in reply as she poured the wine in silence.

Departing the dining room, one of the SEALs blurted out, "How the hell did you know that! That is the most impressive move I have ever seen!"

I answered, "Gentleman, if you cannot identify fragrances, your prospects are indeed limited." Enthusiastic laughter erupted. I found myself an instant celebrity and, for one night, the coolest man in the Middle East.

As the conflicts in the region continued, Skylink became involved in the provision of services in Afghanistan, starting with the transportation of Canadian military personnel from Canada to Kandahar as part of the coalition efforts. The services expanded to in-theater helicopter transportation of civilian contractors. Skylink provided 45 helicopters and flight crews and seven airplanes. The Taliban were active in the Kandahar region, and in July 2009, a rocket-propelled grenade (RPG) shot down a Skylink Ml 26 helicopter with the loss of the entire flight crew of five. A month later, an accident resulted in the loss of an additional helicopter and 13 deaths, including two American contractors.

As I continued to travel over the years, extensively to Asia and Europe, my return to the United States was often interesting as custom officers took note of the "Emergency" visas from Iraq and Sudan on my passport. They were likely curious as to who I was and assumed clandestine US government involvement.

Departing Dubai, I flew to Cairo, then on to Sudan to visit Skylink operations there. Upon landing, I was met at the Khartoum airport by a former Sudanese general who ran Skylink in Sudan. Our interaction was strictly professional. He walked me through security, customs, and immigration. They did not ask me any questions and just waved me through every step without any security checks. It was surreal.

The Skylink office was near the airport, so it took us only a few minutes to get there by car. The building was a fortress. It had glass splinters and razor wire on top of 12-foot walls. It also had steel window shutters bolted shut, leaving nothing for onlookers' imagination. As we were sitting in the late-evening quiet of the office, I asked the general why there were internal steel shutters on the windows. He responded, "This was the hideout of the international terrorist Ramirez Sanchez, known to the world as Carlos the Jackal."

Carlos was born in Caracas, Venezuela, in 1949. He studied in Moscow at Patrice Lumumba University until his expulsion. He converted to Islam in the early 1990s and has claimed credit for eighty murders. The assassin in Frederick Forsyth's *The Day of the Jackal* is based on him. When French agents raided Carlos's safe house in 1975, a copy of the book was found among his belongings, leading to his nom de guerre, Carlos the Jackal. In three of Robert

Ludlum's bestsellers, he based a fictional character known for his cunning, brutality, and deadly terroristic murders on Carlos.

On occasion, Carlos reportedly disguised himself as a priest. His first mission in 1973 was the murder of a prominent Jewish businessman, Joseph Sieff, the president of retailer Marks and Spencer in London. In the early 70s, he joined the PLO and was given the code name Carlos by Abu Sharif.

In January 1975, Carlos led a failed rocket attack on an El Al airliner at Orly airport in Paris. Later in June, his PLO handler, Michel Moukharbal, was arrested and led French police to a flat in Paris, where Carlos welcomed the police and entertained them with drinks before drawing a machine pistol and killing two detectives. He then escaped and fled to Beirut. The same year in December, Carlos and five others stormed the OPEC meetings in Vienna, killing two security guards and capturing more than 60 OPEC officials. Carlos demanded a jet, which he used to fly the hostages to Algiers, where he secured a $50 million ransom.

At the time of the murders of the French policemen in Paris in 1975, Carlos was unknown to authorities. A manhunt ensued to capture or kill him, which lasted for decades. Although the circumstances surrounding his capture in Khartoum, Sudan, have never been fully communicated, he was ultimately taken there alive in 1994. A French court had convicted him of murder in absentia two years earlier. As I sat in the dimly lit Skylink offices, I was processing the deadly evil that had resided within these walls.

I departed Khartoum on a Skylink flight to Darfur, where a civil war was underway. It started in February 2003 when several rebel groups began an armed conflict with the government in the Darfur region of Sudan. Early in the morning on April 25, 2003, the genocide started when the rebels attacked a sleeping government garrison in Al-Fashir. Most of the captured soldiers were executed, and the Sudanese helicopter gunships were destroyed. The government reprisals were primarily an ethnic cleansing of Darfur's non-Arabs, and this action went unreported in the western press. In Brussels, the International Crisis Group estimated that more than

350,000 people were killed or died of starvation in the conflict. My trip to Al-Fashir happened a year after the madness commenced in a world that was on the brink of destruction.

A cease-fire agreement was negotiated in 2004, but it had not been ratified by an influential rebel group, so the genocide was still going on at the time I arrived. The United Nations, in an attempt to avoid a continuation of the killings, supported the African Unity mission's efforts to provide troops to restore order and end the violence. The UN selected Skylink to supply 50 helicopters, maintenance crews, and pilots to the African Unity Peace Force. By 2005, the UN had stationed 7,000 personnel in Darfur to halt the genocide. The cost of this effort was approximately $220 million.

Skylink's goal was to promote peace, prevent war, and to accelerate social well-being. They were often the prime source of reinforcement around the world. It was exciting and a risky business, because one mistake could cost the loss of lives and millions of dollars.

After the trips to Iraq and Sudan, our attorneys and accountants engaged in diligence in preparation to fund and close the transaction. A host of regulatory issues required review and confirmation, considering the sensitive nature of Skylink's operations. A number of premier lenders provided indications of their support to complete the deal. As often occurs in complex transactions, with international requirements, the closing was delayed for nearly two years while my partner Mark Massad and I spent several million dollars of our personal funds on associated accounting and legal fees.

The delay had repercussions that were unimaginable, and then in fall 2008, the financial crisis hit and disabled banks and entire economies around the world. Globally lenders canceled the funding of purchases. Ultimately, we partnered with a preeminent New York–based private equity fund to complete the deal, though with our negotiating leverage stifled due to the withdrawal of banking support, the closing in November 2008 resulted in our loss of a controlling interest.

In 2005, I was contacted by an investment banker in New York, who advised me that he has been engaged to sell Neways, a network seller of cosmetics and nutritional drinks based just south of Provo, Utah. He was aware of my extensive direct-sales experience and management of cosmetics businesses globally. He was looking for an experienced manager potentially interested in such a purchase.

We executed a nondisclosure agreement, secured a host of financial and operational information, and set to work parsing the data. The lead market in Neways's global operations was Japan, and their product line looked strong. I was concerned about certain operational activities, particularly in Japan. The founders were a husband and wife, and the business grew rapidly under their leadership, but they neglected an important business requirement. They failed to pay their taxes. They both went to prison, and the business had to be sold.

After a month of preliminary investigation, we notified the banker that we would not be proceeding or submitting a bid.

Several years after Neways had been purchased by the private equity fund Golden Gate Capital, I was contacted by my friend Jesse Watson, whom I first worked with when he was at CD&R and I was running Jafra. Since that time, Jesse had launched Virgo, his own private equity fund in San Francisco. When he contacted me, I was at Fox Paine, the private equity firm.

Jesse knew John Gilligan, a partner at Golden Gate Capital. Neways's sales were languishing following the business suspension in Japan. Jesse suggested that John call me because I might have some interest in repositioning the company.

A few days later, I was at the Golden Gate offices in San Francisco, where I meet John and several other of the firm's partners. They provided me with a comprehensive overview of Neways. Among the details were the financials and the key operating indicators (KOIs), including detailed information about the independent sales force. Not surprisingly, the number of sales representatives had declined significantly in Japan, after the government-required suspension. Sales were falling in line with the reduction of the sales force.

The restart in Japan had not progressed in the way that the Japanese management team had planned or forecasted. I was offered the opportunity to take over as CEO, which I declined, suggesting that I could be most effective as a Golden Gate consultant representing the financial firm rather than the company. They agreed, and we executed a consultancy agreement.

I said I wanted a week to review the extensive data and prepare a preliminary analysis. This would be followed by a global operations management visit to the company's headquarters in Utah and a trip to Japan for meetings with the Japanese management team.

The materials were revealing, and they indicated that the real challenge resided in reinvigorating the field leadership. I suggested that they engage my friend and Jafra colleague Alan Fearnley in London to work with me on the evaluation and development of an action plan. The key to reestablishing the growth of the field resided in an effective marketing plan, and Alan was the best there was for that assignment. Golden Gate agreed, and Alan and I were back working together. I developed a preliminary plan of action, focused primarily on the field interactions.

Step One was the creation of a sample kit of best-selling Neways products in Japan. Step Two was the creation of an emotional and effective field video. Step Three was large and engaging field meetings in Tokyo, Osaka, and Fukuoka. Step Four was ten small-format meetings throughout Japan with up to 50 leaders at each session. The plan included a number of other suggestions, but these were the drivers.

In 2009 Alan and I made repeated trips to Japan. Alan flew east from London, and I traveled west from LA. Neways had its own video production facility in Utah headed by George Rivera, a wonderful and talented executive. Alan worked closely with George and his team to design a video that was aspirational and emotional and set the right tone. Several Neways executives saw a preview of the video and exclaimed, as did George, that it was the best work they have ever done. Alan and I were staying up in the mountains at Sundance. The ski resort was founded by Robert Redford. It was a bit of a drive daily to the Neways office, but it was an amazing and inspirational venue.

The large meetings were approaching, and we would be in Japan the entire month of September 2009. I booked our rooms at the Ritz-Carlton in Tokyo, a beautiful hotel located in the Roppongi Hills. The hotel lobby was on the 42nd floor, where the elevator opened to a three-story lobby with 360-degree views of Tokyo.

Early on a Sunday morning, I took Alan to a bar in Tokyo where they were showing live the USC-Ohio State football game. It was Saturday evening in California, but we enjoyed the game on Sunday morning with Bloody Marys. The sample products had been completed for the meetings, and they were ready for presentation in the Neways Experience boxes designed by Alan and George. Alan and I asked to be present at the Tokyo Opera House the day before the first large meeting to walk through the rehearsal.

The Japanese management team said they had never rehearsed events, but at our request, they assembled the full production team, including lights, staging, and sound techs. Alan and I sat in the middle of the vast orchestra seating area, and unfortunately, the rehearsal was a disaster. Calmly but firmly, Alan and I advised the local management that no one should plan on leaving. We redid the staging, lighting, and production components and rehearsed the live presentations several times.

When George arrived from Utah, he worked with a stage crew to create an imaginative and engaging display for the reveal of the video and the presentation boxes. It was a long and tiresome process. Eventually we were satisfied, and we sent everyone home well after midnight. The rehearsal of a one-hour show had taken 14 hours. The next evening, three hours before the show was set to kick off, more than a thousand associates were waiting in line to enter. The venue was filled to capacity with more than 3,000 attendees, some standing. The rehearsals paid great dividends, and the show was wonderful.

The associates responded enthusiastically, and, as they left, each was given a Neways Experience box filled with the company's top-selling products. In the coming weeks, we hosted similar shows, to large associate turnouts, in Osaka and Fukuoka. The buzz had started among the field leadership, and immediately following these large events, we began the ten small-format meetings throughout Japan. These meetings included up to 50 field leaders, and following brief remarks by Alan and me and the local management, we had an open-ended Q&A. We stayed as long as they had questions, and each one got answered. In network selling, these leaders represented the key to success. Their trust and support were essential to the growth of the business.

Local management neglected to tell us that during our month-long September stay in Japan there was a silver jubilee holiday. These national holidays were long weekends and observed by all businesses.

When Alan and I discovered that there would be four days of inactivity, we decided to take a break and see some sights. Alan headed to Mt. Fuji to enjoy the natural hot springs in the shadow of the mountain. I went to Bali, but I didn't appreciate the distances involved.

Several friends had shared stories of their experiences in Bali and of the beauty of the beaches and surf. I contacted my friend Kuno, the former head of management at the Four Seasons hotel group. Kuno arranged for me to stay in a beautiful villa with a private courtyard and pool at the Four Seasons. I departed Tokyo following a full day at the Neways office, and after an eight-and-a-half-hour flight, arrived the next morning. I entered the immigration hall and saw large red signs in English that had a skull and crossbones, notifying travelers that the possession of narcotics in Bali is a crime subject to the death penalty. This was another grim reminder that due process and proportionality, which we take for granted in America, is in short supply in many parts of the globe.

My short visit to Bali was wonderful but exhausting because of the flight commitments involved. I returned to Tokyo more tired than when I departed, and we continued the field meetings and presentations.

The results from the meetings and business initiatives were remarkable. The company experienced a 50 percent increase in sales through its associates in the next three months. In my meetings with Golden Gate and the Japanese executive managers prior to the events, I urged them repeatedly that follow-up planning was essential or gains would be rapidly lost. The Japanese management was not supportive. They were a bit embarrassed by our success, considering that they had been unable to grow the business for several years.

Once again, Golden Gate offered me the opportunity to take over the company globally as CEO. Again, I declined. Success could only be achieved with a comprehensive replacement of management in Japan. I accepted their offer to go on the board of directors, where I remained active for two years.

My experience at Neways reinforced the fundamental advice I had been given by Ron Clark at Jafra. The success of network selling was not geared to the product line or packaging. The most valuable asset of these businesses was the field force. Winning their trust and support was the key to success.

Chapter 8

LegalShield

In 2004, Ellen, Taylor, and Charlotte moved to Malibu. I continued to travel back to see my kids every other weekend from my European postings and from New York. They loved my house in Beverly Hills, and when they were there, they lived in the swimming pool. Charlotte frequently brought her friend Ashley with her for the weekend. The trips back and forth to Malibu, though less than 20 miles distant, often took an hour or longer to make the Friday pickup and Sunday evening return.

Taylor enjoyed skiing with me, and during his school vacations or over long weekends, we drove up to Bear Mountain, which was three hours from Beverly Hills. During one of our trips, we were staying in a hotel near the mountain and were startled awake as the building was shaking and swaying. We knew instantly that it was an earthquake. Car alarms sounded throughout the parking lot, and Taylor leapt out of bed, landing on me with a choke hold. The violent moment seemed to last for many minutes—though it was likely 30 seconds—and then it ceased. We heard voices in panic next to our room and turned on our lights, and we saw there was little damage. We quickly recovered after some additional rest and headed over to the mountain for the first runs of the day. I had experienced quakes before in California, but the epicenter of this shaker was right where we were staying in Big Bear Lake.

The next day, we experienced a number of secondary tremors as they hit the mountain. Seeing the slopes move and feeling the motion underfoot while we were skiing was an out-of-body experience.

In Spring 2008, we enjoyed the uncluttered skiing and the beautiful weather, and at 1:00 p.m. on Sunday, we left the mountain to drive back to the house in Beverly Hills, arriving there shortly before 4:00 p.m. Immediately, we changed into our bathing suits and jumped in the pool. There are few places globally where you can ski in the morning and swim in the afternoon. After our swim, I cooked burgers on the grill in my shorts and T-shirt.

Taylor always had a love of music and singing. During his years at Malibu High School (yes, it really does exist), he was a member of the Malibu High chorus, and he was selected by audition to join the elite Chamber Singers, a remarkably talented and dedicated group. They were led by Ms. Mezz (as she was known), a brilliant and demanding instructor, and they regularly won the California state choral competitions. Ms. Mezz had a PhD in choral music and was also the head of that department at UCLA, holding down two full-time assignments. The Chamber Singers performed exceptionally complex sacred music. During Taylor's junior year, Ms. Mezz entered the Chamber Singers in an international choir competition, and they won. The winners were invited to sing at the Easter sunrise service at the Acropolis in Athens, Greece. Two days later, they sang for the Pope in St. Peter's Basilica in Rome.

For his junior and senior high school years, Taylor moved in with me at the house in Beverly Hills.

Malibu High also had an accomplished theatrical department—not surprising given that the parents' association included such notable actors as Mel Gibson and others. Taylor would have been a natural for the singing roles in the musical productions; however, his interests were in staging, sound, lighting, and production. Rehearsals were demanding, often going until 11:00 p.m., following a full day of classes. Taylor had his driver's license by his junior year, but I was concerned about him driving late at night. When I was not traveling for work, I set out late at night to pick him up. On occasion, another Malibu parent, whose daughter was his friend and also a member of the Chamber Singers and a lead singer in the musicals, drove him all the way back to Beverly Hills. Taylor called the mother "Patty."

One morning as we were getting ready for school, he asked me if I had heard of a female rock band singer named Patty. I asked him what her last name was. Benatar, he replied.

A few weeks before Christmas each year, the Malibu choir and the Chamber Singers held a Christmas concert and together they beautifully performed complex compositions written in the 18th and 19th centuries. Each year, seniors auditioned to give a solo performance of a song they selected. Taylor kept it a secret that he had auditioned and had been selected to be featured in this special family evening.

As the day of the performance arrived, I drove to Malibu, with the ticket Taylor had given me. I was stunned to see a line of patrons extending across the school courtyard. Entering, I met Ellen, Taylor, and Charlotte, and Taylor quickly headed backstage as the concert was about to start. Every seat in the enormous performance hall was filled. Unseated students sat on the stairs and between the aisles.

As the evening progressed, the audience was taken by the caliber, intricacy, and complexity of the selections. Finally, as the evening was drawing to a close, several soloists were invited to the large stage, one at a time to share their songs.

Taylor, at 6'4 with his shoulder-length blond hair and wearing a black suit, cut an impressive figure as he walked alone on the stage. Accompanied by a pianist, he sang, "The Christmas Shoes," which was written in 2000 by the Christian vocal group New Song. It recounted a Christmas Eve story of a man completing his last-minute shopping.

In the checkout line and "not really in the Christmas mood," he hears a young boy tell the clerk he doesn't have the money to buy shoes for his terminally ill mother so she will be beautiful when she meets Jesus. The man, suddenly revived with the spirit of Christmas, buys the shoes for him. The song, new to me, was an emotional watershed. As Taylor finished the last note, everyone around the auditorium was in tears and stood up, offering a standing ovation.

A father's pride and the blessing of his son was the best Christmas gift any dad could imagine.

Rip on his Ducati Monster motorcycle Malibu Canyon. 2002

While Taylor stayed with me, I had a simple rule, enforced by all parents: No drinking. One evening sitting together with Charlotte and Taylor, we talked about this, and I told them that their safety was what truly mattered. I made them an offer they couldn't refuse.

"Though drinking is dangerous and irresponsible, I want you to know that you can call me at any time, day or night," I said. "If you or a friend have been drinking, I will come and pick you up—no questions asked."

A year later, when Taylor was 18 years old, and during the spring of his senior year, I returned late on a flight from London to Los

Angeles. At 2:00 a.m., the phone rang. It was Taylor. "Dad, I don't think I should drive home," he said.

I asked for the address, which was high up in the hills of the Pacific Palisades, and I got up, dressed quickly, and drove half an hour to retrieve him. I thanked him for the call, and we drove home quietly. We didn't discuss it again for 10 years.

Charlotte started third grade in the Malibu schools, following one year in Westlake Village. Though her brother's interests were focused on the choir, Chamber Singers, and play productions, she enjoyed an ease and ability in generating new friendships. Despite the displacement at an important and young age, she gathered new friends to her without effort, and she still has many of those relationships today.

Malibu High School had a curious weekly schedule, with every Friday being a half day of classes, and the students were dismissed at noon. This schedule had been ostensibly created to allow professional development for the teachers, but these Friday afternoons were also set aside for extra instruction for any students requiring extra help. In practice, the school parking lot was a desert at 12:15 p.m., on Fridays. Char and I gathered every Friday we could for lunch at Sugarfish, our favorite sushi restaurant. Sometimes, it was only the two of us dining, but more often than not, she brought six or more of her friends. It was marvelous, and I got to know these young women over many years, and they spoke openly and with ease when I was around. On a typical Friday I was entertained for more than an hour as they shared stories of teachers, other friends, and, of course, boys.

Their openness was refreshing, the stories were frequently amusing, and their laughter was contagious.

In 2008, when I was least expecting, I was introduced to Diana, a wonderful woman from Orange County. She was recently divorced with two children, including a very young daughter. She was an entrepreneur and had built her career from scratch. Her father had been a helicopter pilot in the Vietnam War, and he served three tours. Not many helicopter pilots survived the war, and fewer served that many tours. It was an impressive feat that not many soldiers were able to achieve.

Sadly, Diana's dad, her hero, died in his 40s, shortly after his return from Vietnam. Following his death, Diana put herself through college and became a computer programmer, ultimately running her own company for many years.

Diana and I dated for several months and enjoyed our time together. But the challenges of my business travel and the distance from where I was living in LA to Orange County where she was proved overwhelming. It was impossible to just get together for a quick dinner or a movie. Also, we were both overcoming the issues of recent divorce with children in tow. Taking note of all variables, we determined that it would be best to move on and go our separate paths, so we said our farewells.

In the summer of 2010, after stepping off the board at Neways, I began working with Steve Rusch, a former Merrill Lynch investment banker, to submit an offer to acquire Neways, together with another network business also headquartered in Utah. Steve and I had worked closely together several years earlier as we received inquiries to purchase Jafra. Significant work goes into preparing the strategic business case and combined financial forecast for an acquisition like this.

We set up several meetings in New York with private equity firms I'd worked with previously and where we already had relationships. One of these funds, MidOcean Partners, was formally known as Deutsche Bank Private Equity. They were an independent fund with a number of terrific companies in their portfolio. Seven years earlier, Deutsche Bank Private Equity initiated an offer to buy Jafra. I knew several of their partners from when we visited Jafra operations in the United States, Mexico, and Europe.

Steve and I arrived at the MidOcean offices on Park Avenue and were taken into a conference room where I meet Frank Schiff and Noah Rabinsky. Also joining the meeting was Daniel Penn. I walked the team through the presentation, sharing insights and observations from my time at Neways. They were familiar with the success of the Jafra operations and investment. As I concluded the presentation, Frank asked, "Are you familiar with Pre-Paid Legal, a network company based in Oklahoma?"

I responded that I was familiar with the company and that it provided customers with affordable legal advice in exchange for a monthly subscription price. I was not aware of the company's performance, and I had never met their founder or executive team. I did not believe they participated in the Direct Selling Association meetings.

Frank, who became a good friend, asked if I was interested in looking at the business because MidOcean was starting diligence, with the intention of submitting a bid to acquire the company. Noah, who also became a good friend, said his mother was a Pre-Paid Independent Associate.

Noah's knowledge of the service plan had struck a chord at Mid Ocean and prompted them to learn more about the business. They did not have anyone on their executive team who had experience with network sales companies, and I would be a terrific addition. Pre-Paid Legal was a New York Stock Exchange publicly held company. A sales process had begun with the appointment of a special committee of the board to solicit and review offers. The company had co-CEOs after its founder, Harland Stonecipher, stepped down recently following a family tragedy and several health concerns.

MidOcean brought me on to work on the diligence efforts, and they sent over extensive financial and operational information for me to review. My preliminary read was that the company had been languishing for several years. Earnings were strong, but their compensation plan resulted in elevated profitability as new sales declined. This counterintuitive result occurs as the company offers an insurance business–like commission, where the seller of a membership is advanced an entire year of premiums in the month of sale.

I also noted that field compensation was actually declining as corporate profitability increased. The decline in commissions was geared to charge-backs against selling associates if a membership canceled in the first year after the associate had received the annual commission. I was surprised that this field compensation plan had not been routinely shared with an emphasis on retaining sold memberships in order to protect commissions. In network selling vocabulary, the commission paid to independent associates is known as the compensation plan. When we took over Jafra from Gillette, the compensation plan has not been amended for more than 20 years, and during our six years managing the company, we never revised it.

The Pre-Paid Legal compensation plan had been changed at least six times in the previous four years. Not only had this created confusion in the field and with the company's financial results, but the company had routinely offered bonus incentives above the commission structure that were based on enhanced sales goals and rewarded monthly, which frequently resulted in poor-quality subscriptions.

Frank, Noah, and I were joined by MidOcean partner Elias Dokas and operating affiliate Frank Sowinski. The five of us traveled several times to the corporate headquarters in Ada, OK, in the south-central part of the state. We all flew to the Dallas airport and drove three hours to Ada. Crossing the Red River, cellular service and radio signals often disappear. Frank, ever with a lead foot, was always determined to beat his best time for the drive.

The diligence meetings with management were held in the evenings after the employees had left for the day. Accommodations in Ada were limited, and we usually stayed at the Holiday Inn Express, which offered breakfast with the room. I met Frank for coffee and discussed the work for the day. One morning after a late-night checkin, Frank told me that after he picked up his key and went up to his room, he opened the door and found a man sitting on the bed in his underwear.

"Did you ask him which side of the bed he wanted to sleep on?" I asked Frank.

The meetings were a great opportunity for us to meet the management team and assess the company's abilities and challenges. One night we drove to Dallas for dinner before an early-morning flight home the next day. At dinner, Frank asked, "Are you ready to run this business? You've drawn the short straw."

Everyone had a laugh at my expense as I agreed to come in as CEO. I told Frank I was not going to move from Beverly Hills to Ada, which led to additional laughter. Frank noted that I would have the only Bentley in Ada.

I agreed to the offer as long as we opened an executive office in Dallas and that I could bring along Alan Fearnley as president to run marketing and sales. Frank and the team readily agreed. Bids were submitted, and we proceeded to the second round. I was determined to have discussions with field leaders to get their views of the company, its operations, opportunities, and disappointments. A series of phone interviews were set up with a half dozen top associate leaders.

A minder from the company was on all these calls, but my questions were not limited. Frank and Noah also listened in, but they did not participate in the Q&A. The leaders were enthusiastic and committed. They were clearly engaged and supportive of the business. What I did not know at the time was that a major schism in the business was looming.

Our MidOcean team worked through the 2010 Christmas holidays on the diligence review. I visited Ada several times and met with Pre-Paid Legal founder Harlan Stonecipher and his wife Shirley. The corporate campus was exceptional. I was impressed with the operational team and, in particular, Pre-Paid Legal customer service headed by Linda Brown. The company had more than 350 customer service specialists, and their training was extensive and unlike the many customer service installations I had managed previously. At Pre-Paid Legal, there were no digital displays supplying key real-time information.

When I asked Linda why this information was not available to the team, she smiled and noted that at Pre-Paid Legal, the secret sauce was open-ended customer engagement. The service plans were somewhat complex, particularly for new members. They tried never to rush a call or to leave a member frustrated. Linda and her team of supervisors have real-time displays on their desks. If call queues or talk times become too long, they would intervene to expedite. This simple yet elegant approach to best-in-class customer service earned the respect of new members and field leadership. The customer service wing had been constructed on long but relatively narrow floors. Unlike other customer service installations that were typically in large windowless conference centers, no customer service representative at Pre-Paid Legal was more than 30 feet from a window and sunlight. A brilliant concept.

I always had lunch or dinner with Harlan and Shirley when I visited corporate headquarters, and he was complimentary of my success at Jafra and asked about my business philosophies, with his great western charm. "These businesses are all about the field," I responded. "Understanding them, knowing them by name, and taking the time to understand their goals, strengths, and weaknesses. Their trust is the key to the success of the business."

Harlan smiled and commented, "You really understand this and what the drivers are."

Final bids were prepared and submitted in January 2011. There was jockeying among the bidders, and our strongest case was our superior understanding of network selling and field relationships. I had learned this fundamental notion years earlier from my friend Ron Clark, and this won us Harlan's support. He was the company's largest stockholder, and his endorsement was important.

On Sunday, January 23, Frank and Noah called to tell me we had won the bid, and I needed to be in Ada the next morning for a national announcement and for Harland to introduce me to the field and employees. I left from LAX late that afternoon, knowing that a snowstorm was forecast in central Oklahoma the next day. The rental car representatives in Oklahoma City proudly told me they had reserved a new Lincoln Continental for me. I noted that a four-wheel-drive SUV might be a better choice, considering the forecast.

This turned out to be a good decision. After a few hours of sleep, I arrived at the corporate headquarters and was taken to the executive floor, where Harlan and his team were waiting. A short time later, the national broadcast kicked off, with Harlan graciously congratulating me and recounting our lunches and dinners. He carefully walked listeners through my résumé and said, "This is a man who understands network selling."

To my surprise, before he asked me to make a few remarks, Harlan announced that I would be taking over immediately as the head of the business. The closing of the purchase was many months off because financing and regulatory approvals were required. I had expected a multi-month transition, but I also understood it was time to be agile and learn on the job. A number of field leaders, including Dave Savula, the company's number one selling associate, also offered their congratulations and endorsement. We went down to the first-floor auditorium, a beautiful multilevel theater, where Harlan had gathered more than 500 employees. After his generous introduction, I pledged to focus on learning the culture of the business and being respectful of the amazing company created by Harlan and the management team. I closed by saying that our plans must constantly focus our efforts on the field.

Ron would be proud.

After a series of additional meetings and conference calls, I departed Ada shortly before midnight, headed for Dallas. It was starting to snow, and I quickly saw I was the only driver on the road. As I kept going, the snow picked up and combined with sleet. Soon I had lost my cell phone reception. I kept the radio on to help me stay awake and to provide some company. Eventually the signal dropped out, and even though I pressed the search button for other stations, I watched the radio scan over and over without picking up a signal. It occurred to me that I was "off the grid," and this was not a good time for a road mishap.

At 3:00 a.m., I arrived at the Mansion on Turtle Creek in Dallas, and the clerk had left a room key on the counter. The snow and sleet continued, and the roads were covered. I set the alarm for 6:00 a.m. to get to the Dallas airport to fly to Los Angeles, but when I woke up, I could hear the sleet hammering against the windows. I went back to sleep, knowing there would be no flights in or out of Dallas that day.

Multiple corporate efforts were underway simultaneously, and I discovered quickly from the field that the repeated revisions of the Pre-Paid Legal compensation plan had generated even more confusion and frustration than I had anticipated.

Several of the special bonus awards had not been paid because renegade associates had submitted phantom memberships to qualify. Also, Harlan's health issues in recent years had kept him from being able to provide a corporate presence in the field. I set up meetings for the top field leaders in Dallas and flew in approximately 50 of them to meet Alan and me and to have open discussions. In a word, they were dispirited, and many had seen a decline in their associate base and a reduction of income because of bad business written and associated charge-backs against commissions.

They loved the service plan, the customer service, and the legacy established by Harlan and Shirley. Alan and I took this fundamental first step in providing them with an open and unfiltered opportunity to vent. We wanted to let them know we needed and valued their input. We realized how much work needed to be done to build back their trust and respect and what a long and difficult process it would be.

We developed a three-prong strategy to demonstrate a fresh approach to the business dedicated to the field. Alan focused on creating a new name and branding. Pre-Paid Legal had been used for 45 years, and it was dated and connoted a less-than-premium service in current usage. We brought in Decision Analyst, a top research company owned and run by Jerry Thomas, to undertake a marketing and branding study, which confirmed our suspicions. The new name had to include type fonts, design, and colors. More than 200,000 independent field sales associates had a close connection and affection for the name Pre-Paid Legal. It was imperative that we tread lightly and get the name change right. We had only one chance.

Late one night, Alan and I were having dinner after a long day at the office, and I told him that if we messed up the new name selection, we might end up driving for Greyhound. We both laughed at the gallows humor.

Normally, a process like this, involving tens of thousands of combinations of names, colors, logos, and fonts, could take up to a year or longer. We had less than three months because our goal was to announce the new name in a video that would be presented to the field at the Dallas convention, being held in September at the American Airline Arena, where the Dallas Mavericks played. More than 12,000 associates would be present for our first show and production for them. The first impression we made would be a key to our future success.

The second prong was to schedule 13 small meetings with the field leadership across the United States and Canada. I was taking a successful page from our Neways playbook. I had noted an absence of engagement by the field, and I wanted them to meet us and connect us with a new direction and dedication to them and their success. More than 95 percent of the independent associates would be directly linked to these few hundred leaders we met with at these small events. Their support of our efforts was essential.

The format of these meetings was important, and Alan and I prepared a brief 30-minute presentation. We openly shared the company's financial results, the decline in commissions, and the rise in chargebacks. The correction was immediately evident to them—retention of memberships. They had never been offered such a candid review and presentation, and many of them were stunned at our accessibility. We then opened up the meeting for Q&A, and at each of these meetings, we stayed for hours until every question was asked and answered. No members of the previous management team were present. This was about us, about a new direction. We were agents of change. In my remarks, I told them that in network selling, the company does well only if the field does well. We were their partners.

Through the spring of 2011, as we worked with MidOcean on the transaction financing and assorted regulatory approvals, Alan and I visited a number of major market events. At these weekend gatherings, we had a chance to speak to local leaders and enjoyed getting to know them.

Dave Savula was the company's leading money earner, and he was a legend. He had been an independent leader with LegalShield for nearly 20 years. The first time I heard him speak was when Alan and I attended a southern California meeting in Irvine, CA. Dave was exceptionally witty, self-deprecating, and he commanded the room of nearly a thousand that showed up to hear from him. When Dave called me to the front of the room, I thanked him, noting from the heart that he was the best I had ever seen.

Several weeks later, Alan and I appeared with Dave at an event in South Carolina. He invited us to join him and his wife Bev for a weekend of relaxing at their island home off the coast. As Dave drove us down to their home, he entertained us for several hours, and we all laughed a lot.

Bev arranged a barbecue for us that evening. Alan and I had spent the last several months dining out and moving constantly from one hotel to another. This visit was a gift and allowed us to unwind.

I got up early the next morning to go for a run on the beach, and Alan followed me down. Alan was an exceptional swimmer, and whenever a pool was offered, he started doing laps, sometimes for up to an hour at a time. The draw of the ocean was too much for him to resist.

As we approached the shoreline, we saw a few early-morning fisherman surf casting. I took off for my run while Alan slipped on goggles and headed into the water. When I returned, I looked out into the water and Alan was a tiny spec a good 200 yards offshore, swimming back and forth parallel to the beach. He swam back in sometime later and approached one of the fishermen and asked, "What are you fishing for today?"

The response: "Sharks."

As our city visits continued across the United States and Canada, we had a meeting scheduled in Chicago during Memorial Day weekend. Alan and I were flying there from Toronto. We reached the departure area and were told that thunderstorms in Chicago were delaying the departure by several hours. Alan and I found a restaurant, where the Indy 500 was being shown on the television. My friend and race car driver Oriol Servia was racing, and he was in first place for several hours. One of his cars was parked in my driveway in Beverly Hills. As the hours passed and the delays increased, I called the field leader in Chicago who was coordinating our appearance and suggested postponement. They wanted to go ahead with the meeting as the buzz was already circulating from earlier meetings around the country. Our flight departed eight hours late, and when we landed at O'Hare, all the gates were occupied. We taxied out to a holding area, with little communication from the aircrew, and waited for hours more.

We arrived at the meeting twelve hours late, and unbelievably the field leaders were still waiting for us. I had called every hour and suggested they depart, but they declined. It was after midnight, and we were greeted enthusiastically with applause. We had not had time to change into suits and walked in wearing jeans and pulling our luggage and sorely in need of a shower. The meeting was a success and became a legend in company history.

The third and vital undertaking was to revisit and reconstruct the field compensation plan. This was a daunting task with abundant opportunities for missteps and errors. The comp plan, as it was known, was the single most important factor driving field behaviors, and it can be geared to drive the recruitment of new associates. Alternatively, comp plans can be directed to reward sales or other activities—and yet there was a limit on the dollars to be allocated. Once again, the repeated changes to the plan had been a disaster, and we had no alternative to getting this right and putting it to bed. Certainty and finality were required—as was attaining the complete buy-in by the top field leadership. These determinations would have an impact on their personal earnings of millions of dollars in the years ahead.

The program coding to amend these plans was exceptional. Each component of the revisions to the plan had to be back tested for years of actual sales to validate that there would be no anomalies that could be disastrous for the business. As CEO, I determined how we approached this. I had the clear authority to develop a new plan internally and mandate it to the field. Time was getting short, and this was the most efficient manner to proceed. Instead, I convened a group of approximately 17 field leaders to work with me directly on this project. My assistant, Melanie Lawson, was invaluable in these efforts. Melanie was a star and the company's resident comp specialist.

I hosted a series of all-day meetings at various venues around the country. Each aspect of the current plan was examined in excruciating detail, and the leaders openly debated the direction and appropriate revisions. Their involvement was right out of Ron Clark's playbook. They had never been afforded the visibility of these financial metrics or invited to openly submit their proposals. I was slowly building trust and a following among them that would transfer to their downline associates.

I selected two prominent leaders, Larry Smith and Patrick Shaw, as the primary field representatives to work closely with Melanie and me. Larry was a 20-year PrePaid Legal leader with a commitment to the value of the membership plan. He was a member of Dave Savula's team. Dave was the company's top associate, earning more than $2 million annually. Patrick, a leader for approximately 10 years, was more directed to recruitment. He was a member of the Jeff Olson team, which merged with Pre-Paid Legal. Their biases in approach (membership versus recruitment) reflected the direction of their leadership.

Alan and I were working with the senior corporate staff seven days a week, providing them with daily updates on each of the initiatives. The MidOcean team flew in once a month.

Dave Savula and Jeff Olson were the senior field leaders in their organizations, and they were in great demand for appearances at monthly meetings. These gatherings, known as Super Saturdays, were held throughout the country and in Canada.

LegalShield
Convention
Las Vegas.
2014

As the new CEO, I received a host of invitations to speak at the events and putting a face and voice on new management showed our conviction to field service. On a typical Friday evening, I flew out of Dallas and returned on Saturday night or on Sunday. On numerous occasions, I joined Dave or Jeff if they were presenting. I was also joined at meetings and presentations by Darnell Self, Michael Humes, Larry and Doni Smith, Nick and Gayle Serba, and other top leaders. These gatherings provided opportunities for one-on-one dinners following a full day of meetings.

As the comp plan efforts were coming together, I met with Dave and Jeff, who offered helpful suggestions and gave their approval. The final step was to present the plan to the deal team at MidOcean in New York. The cultural nuances of the plan, behaviors influenced, and the intended financial consequences were of immeasurable importance. Dave and Jeff accompanied Melanie and me to the meeting, where we faced precise questioning. But we adjourned with consensus, and the plan was good to go.

In most network businesses, management presents the comp plan to the field. For the Dallas event in September, I elected an alternative course and asked Larry and Patrick to present the new plan to the attendees. I wanted to have their personal views and excitement influence the crowd. This would prove to be a great call because they were exceptional on the stage—exciting, often humorous, and engaging, and the field responded enthusiastically.

In early June, just when we thought we were making progress, the bottom fell out. It was right in front of us, and we never saw it coming. I received a call in my Dallas office from John Hoffman, an exceptional leader in Jeff Olson's side of the business. John's wife Darcy was a gifted marketing and training professional. She was a PhD and had authored several notable books. Alan and I had held one of the earlier small leadership gathering events with them in Tennessee.

John said a matter had come up, and he needed to speak with me about it immediately. I responded that we could talk then, but John said it was too important for a phone call and he would fly to Dallas the next day to meet with me.

I met John the next morning at the Dallas airport. He began by saying that deciding to contact me was one of the most difficult choices he had made in his career. He had spoken to his pastor about it. He said he could not live with himself without making me aware of information he had received. Jeff Olson was leaving Pre-Paid Legal to start his own network marketing company.

Jeff's new business would launch in September, immediately following our Dallas convention. The new company would offer a specialized skin-care line. My background in cosmetics made me realize immediately that these efforts had been underway for well over a year. The formulation of skin care is demanding and involves extensive product testing. The design and selection of packaging and marketing materials takes up to six months more if you are very experienced.

John and I barely knew each other then, but over the next few years, I became close friends with John and Darcy. Their generosity and the support of associates from other organizations was something unique to the company. Their daughter Brielle was a rising star in the business, and I was so proud of her. I began to feature her at national events. Many years later, John officiated at my wedding to Diana.

My immediate concern about Jeff was who might leave with him. The next day, I let Frank and Noah know what was happening and flew to Fort Lauderdale to meet with Jeff. In calm and measured tones, I told him I had heard about his intentions to launch a new business. Jeff was aware of my extensive cosmetics background, and I told him I knew the launch of this business was a multiple-year effort.

He did not disagree. Left unsaid was my disappointment in learning about it at this late juncture with so much time and effort already invested. Jeff was fully cognizant of my legal background. In closing, I noted that he was entirely free to pursue alternative business interests, but I cautioned that under the Pre-Paid Legal associate agreement, which he and all his team members had signed, no one could recruit an associate to join another company. We shook hands, and I departed for Dallas. I spend the next several days on calls with Frank and Noah and surveyed other top leaders to determine if they were involved with Jeff's new business.

A week or two after I learned this news about Jeff, I hosted a dinner at my home in Beverly Hills and invited Dave Savula, Darnell Self, Brian Carruthers, and Mark Smith and his wife Tammy. Other than Dave, all of them were members of Jeff's organization, and they had known him for more than a decade. A noted Italian chef prepared the meal, and individual invitations were prepared with each person's name on the top of the page. We dined on my patio overlooking the canyons below Mulholland Drive. Unfortunately, Dave was unable to attend. We had a wonderful evening, and after dinner, we headed inside for a brief discussion about the ramifications of Jeff's departure. They all expressed surprise and were upset.

As we entered the summer months, we had five finalists for a new company name. Each required trademark and copyright searches to validate that they were available. We presented the names at a MidOcean deal team meeting at the Mansion on Turtle Creek, and decision analysis commenced, with significant research to determine the most resonant selection. We each put $100 into a pot, and the team member who selected the name we ended up with would take home the prize.

We planned to announce the new name at the convention in Dallas that September, and Alan was already working on a script for a video that would reveal the new name. Our days were full, with little sleep and no weekends for rest. Our closing to buy the company was coming up in August as regulatory approvals were secured.

Once the closing took place in August and everything was official, it was once again time to burn the boats and move to Dallas. I had recently remodeled my home in Beverly Hills, in a small gated community off Benedict Canyon called Wallingford Estates. My next-door neighbors were Bob Shapiro and his family, along with Seal and Heidi Klum. I reluctantly put the house on the market, and it sold quickly to an executive and his family relocating from New York. The contract included a two-week closing for me to get ready to move, but much of that time, I was in Oklahoma at the Pre-Paid Legal headquarters. In the final week before the house sale, I faced multiple challenges. Charlotte was starting school in San Francisco, and Taylor was beginning his junior year at Syracuse University, with an off-campus enrollment at their LA facility.

I had one week to arrange for an apartment for Taylor, get Charlotte settled in San Francisco, and pack up a lifetime's belongings for shipment to Dallas. Somehow all these things happened, and I was back in Ada in five or six days. The new offices in Dallas were under construction, and Alan and I took up residence at the Mansion on Turtle Creek.

With the convention in Dallas approaching, we were in full preparation. Alan scripted an excellent show, which we reviewed numerous times. We shared it with Darnell, who had become a trusted confidant. We kept the new company name a secret.

During the first day of the convention, I invited Alan to the stage to present the new company name in the form of an engaging and emotional video. At that moment, we were the only ones who had seen it. Alan and I took our seats with our partners from MidOcean. Dave and Bev Savula were seated to one side of me. Taylor had flown in for the convention, and he was seated on my other side. The lights went down, and the video began, revealing at the end—LegalShield.

A roar went up from 12,000 attendees. Dave had tears in his eyes, and Bev was grabbing her handkerchief. Frank and Noah were—on their feet. Alan's daughter Ellen had joined us from London. The respect in everyone's eyes made the sleepless nights and 90-hour work weeks worth the effort.

Taylor and I left the arena and headed over to a hotel for lunch.

Walking in, Mike, Kim, and Steve Melia—field leaders who had become good friends—ushered us to their table. The entire restaurant rose in a standing ovation as we took our seats. Taylor was beaming, and I was so thankful he was there with me for this special moment. The Dallas convention was an overwhelming success. Our efforts and the quality of the production were graciously acknowledged by the field. To close the meetings, we played the video one more time for the enthusiastic crowd. As Alan and I departed the arena, we were met by a line of associates wanting to introduce themselves, take photos, and get autographs. We spent time with every one of them, and three hours later, we were exhausted.

The next day included breakout sessions for the major leadership organizations, and I made the circuit speaking at six or more events. At each one, the leaders were congratulatory and effusive in their praise. New friendships were blooming, and we were ready to face Jeff's departure with the conviction and support of the field.

Just as it appeared we had put that difficult matter behind us, the second shoe dropped. Mark Smith called me the day after the convention. I had provided headline stage time for Mark and his wife Tammy during the convention. Mark was the field leader of LegalShield's operations in California, our biggest market in the country. He called to tell me he was leaving to join Jeff Olson. We were leaderless in California.

This likely meant that other leaders were preparing to depart as well. I called Darnell and Alan, and we immediately put together an action plan to support the California market. Within days, we were in Los Angeles, hosting a meeting near the airport that was attended by nearly 800 people. Our message was not on the departures. It was focused on the future—on the value of the membership plan, on the opportunities to develop wealth for families.

Darnell, who was a member of Jeff's organization, was magnificent. He declared his unwavering commitment to LegalShield and assured the room that he and his family would never depart. His oratory was mesmerizing and its effects contagious. I realized that I was in the presence of greatness.

The year 2011 was busy, and while I was getting LegalShield launched, connected with that was a new fascination for me: race car driving. In early June 2011, I met with my friend Mike Ager and Indy race car driver Oriol Servia, both of whom were PrePaid Legal associates. A week or two earlier, over Memorial Day weekend, Oriol had driven in the Indianapolis 500. His 30-lap lead during the race made driving history. I would come to understand that tactics are as important as speed to a race's outcome. The team strategies take into consideration multiple factors, including gas consumption, timing of pit stops, and tire selections for different conditions.

Following Oriol's sustained lead in the 2011 Indy, JR Hildebrand moved ahead of him for the closing laps of the 500-mile race. Unbelievably, in the final lap, on turn 4 with the finish line in sight, Hildebrand lost control of his car, hit the wall, and British driver and former Indy 500 winner Dan Wheldon won the race. Dan was a beloved driver and fan favorite, but he had not driven in any other Indy car races that season. The crowd loved his win.

Oriol and Mike were enthusiastic PrePaid Legal associates and suggested a corporate sponsorship of Oriol's Indy car for the rest of the 2011 season. Oriol was an engineer and a Spaniard with impeccable English. He was a racing legend, and we quickly became great friends. Soon after this meeting, Alan and I were Oriol's guests at an Indy car series race in Dallas and the gala reception after. I also joined Oriol and Mike at the Indy races in Long Beach, CA; St. Petersburg, FL; and Baltimore, MD. At each race, I was invited into the pit and watched the race from ground level. The sound and speed were electrifying.

The high-speed ballet and tight choreography of tire changes performed by the pit crews 10 feet in front of me was stunning and left me breathless. Coverage of this on television was excellent, but the sheer power and sensory input of actual race conditions were overwhelming. I quickly became a race fan. Oriol introduced me to a host of drivers and team owners. His girlfriend Jackie (now his wife) was also a constant companion in the pits. She and I stood talking on the edge throughout each race as Oriol passed in front of us at speeds up to 220 miles per hour.

The 2011 Indy car season closed in October with a final race at the Las Vegas Motor Speedway. This racetrack, redesigned in 2006 for NASCAR events, had not been used for Indy car races since 2000. It has a banked oval design to accommodate the slower NASCAR vehicles that do not have the downdraft of the highly aerodynamic, open-wheel Indy cars. NASCAR competitors with large covered-wheel car bodies often hit one another during every race, but the mere touching of open wheels in the light Indy cars can lead instantaneously to loss of control and result in a car becoming airborne.

Mike Ager, along with his sister Nikita, and I had dinner each night with Oriol and Jackie as the qualifications for this race were underway. Earlier, in May, Indy car CEO Randy Bernard had announced that a $5 million purse would be awarded to any driver who won who was not on the year's Indy car race circuit and who was starting from the back of the field. Oriol enjoyed an exceptional qualifying run and started in second position behind his friend Tony Kanaan.

Dan Wheldon, after his spectacular final lap victory at the Indy 500 on Memorial Day weekend, was a racing commentator for Versus (now NBCSN). Dan was a natural and impressed the Versus execs and race fans. As this final event of the 2011 season neared, Dan was unexpectedly picked up to drive in the race.

The evening before the race, during dinner, Oriol expressed his concern. The lighter, high-downforce Indy cars cannot slide in the corners of the high-banked NASCAR-configured track. At race time, I was in the pit with Oriol's crew, Jackie, Nikita, and Michael. The crowd was joyous with the sound of the cars on the pre-race laps. We were on the edge of the track as the race kicked off in a crescendo of sound. Oriol maintained a lead position, and the excitement was contagious. On lap 11, with the cars directly in front of us and at maximum speed of 220 mph, heading into turn 1, Wade Cunningham, Wheldon's teammate, clipped the tire of James Hinchcliffe, causing Cunningham's car to swerve in front of Wheldon, whose car drove over the rear of Cunningham's and went completely airborne for more than 300 feet and into one of the safety net poles.

Fifteen cars piled into one another at unbelievable speeds, and it was instant chaos. Fires erupted in less than a second. Jackie screamed next to me, and she was hysterical and inconsolable. I told her that Oriol's car was ahead of the crash, and a few minutes later, he passed in front of us on the return lap. As Oriol later described the scene, he thought there had been a terrorist strike in the track tunnel. The multiple fires and scattered debris looked like the scene of an explosion. Helicopters arrived as drivers were being pulled from their cars. There were more fires than safety crews available on the track.

Several drivers were trapped in their crushed race cars, and a number of cars were engulfed in flames. Pandemonium spread across the track and in the pits. Many of the race crews, wives, and friends were in tears. More than an hour later, another helicopter arrived to take Dan Wheldon's wife to the hospital. All the race teams were taken to an emergency meeting at the track media center. Dan had died from his injuries.

As the 2012 Indy car season approached, the series introduced a new and safer car. Dan Wheldon had been a test driver when the new frame system was under design and testing.

At LegalShield there was much excitement about the coming season. Oriol attended several events with me, and we again cosponsored his car. The LegalShield logo was now proudly displayed on the side of his race car, and he wore the logo on the front of his helmet.

Indianapolis 500 LegalShield Indy car driver Oriol Servia. 2012

For the Indy Grand Prix in Baltimore in early September, I invited Darnell, his wife Traci, and several of his top leaders, including Mike Humes, Kevin Mack, and Carlo Brown, to the race. Oriol and his team took us through the setup of his car, and I was invited to the team meeting for the race strategy discussion.

As a surprise the night before the race, Oriol pulled me aside and said he had arranged the two-seat Indy car for me to ride in with Mario Andretti before the race. This ceremonial lap of the course at full speed was a crowd favorite tradition, featuring one lucky fan along for the adventure with the former Indy 500 winner and racing legend.

I called my friend Mike Humes and invited him to meet me at the racetrack three hours before the race.

When he arrived, I informed him that he was in for the ride of a lifetime and gave him my seat in the race car. Mike was speechless. A short while later, he was in a full race suit and helmet and climbing into the car.

As the Indy car races moved across the United States and Canada, I invited top local LegalShield leaders to join me. Social media lit up as many of the leaders had thousands of followers. An invitation to an Indy race, a tour of the pits, and a meet-and-greet with Oriol and the race team became much coveted. At each race, I gave Indy car shirts and hats to our associates. Our sponsorship continued for several seasons, even after Oriol stepped down as our driver.

For four Indy racing seasons, Mike Humes and I traveled to Indianapolis for the Memorial Day 500-mile race. We appeared together at the local Super Saturday LegalShield event the day before the race. This meeting, hosted by exceptional LegalShield leaders Keith and Carol Dickens, was always terrific. Associates traveled from Chicago, Kentucky, and throughout the Midwest for the event, which grew bigger every year. Michael Humes, a former postal deliveryman, was a gifted LegalShield leader and presenter. He was making more than a half-million dollars a year with LegalShield. His personal story was inspirational.

LegalShield had a large IT group of 120 full-time staff members, most of whom directed their efforts at tracking the commission plan and payments to more than 300,000 independent sales associates. These commissions were paid daily via direct deposit.

Our legal services plan provided coverage of more than four million individuals, while the identity theft program, the second largest in the United States, covered more than two million members. When we purchased the company in August 2011, the monthly membership fees had not been increased in nearly 25 years. In the meantime, costs had increased significantly.

In early 2012, I brought together various members of my executive team and several field leaders to discuss an increase in fees. As anticipated, there was significant pushback—from all quarters. I also wanted to initiate an online web service that would allow individuals and families to purchase a membership directly from the company. I knew this proposal would appear to be in direct conflict with the independent associate sales, and I put together a plan with selected sales leaders based on three concepts:

Most online purchasers do not want to work with a third party and were unlikely to respond to a direct sales appeal from a LegalShield associate. I fell into that category and preferred to buy direct online. I believed we were losing sales to the type of buyer who would not purchase from one of our associates.

Our top sales leaders nationally belonged to a group known as Performance Club, and they qualified for special bonuses and exceptional all-expenses-paid trips. There were 800 qualifiers. During my term of leadership, I took them, along with their spouses or significant others, to amazing locations such as Maui, Dana Point, and Cabo San Lucas. LegalShield paid the complete cost of airfares, hotels, transfers, all meals, and entertainment. We booked the entire hotel. Taking into account the online sale of memberships, I wanted to create a fund where a portion of the membership fees were distributed to Performance Club qualifiers. This rewarded them as our sales partners and provided an incentive for new associates to achieve qualification.

Finally, the company would invest in the creation of a new and fresh website designed to attract membership candidates. This investment and creative marketing would accelerate LegalShield's name recognition and company awareness, which would ultimately benefit the selling associates.

As we moved into the summer months of 2012, anxiety had built up among the field leadership and my c-suite executives regarding these parallel and untested initiatives. Every weekend, I continued to travel around the country, promoting the value of the membership and the need to adopt online technology to support our name recognition. The increase in the monthly price and the online membership program were announced simultaneously while everyone held their breath. The day of the announcement, I had a national broadcast that was listened to by more than 10,000 sales associates. Darnell Self had been involved in both initiatives, and I enlisted him for the broadcast so he could endorse them.

The results were even better than expected. Despite fears among my management team, there was no churn off of members. Indeed, member subscriptions surged along with the qualification of new Performance Club members.

Once again, exceptional planning and direct partnership with the independent field leadership swayed the day. And again, Ron Clark's advice resonated in the moment.

Mike Humes and I had shared the stage together at one of my first LegalShield events in Orlando, FL, and our connection was immediate. With more than a thousand people in the audience, Mike took the stage carrying a large glass jar full of marbles. Mike is a single parent. He said each marble represented a weekend day with his beloved daughter Mikayla from the date of her birth until her 18th birthday. He dipped into the jar and extracted several handfuls of marbles. The marbles left served as a countdown to her adulthood.

He took out two more marbles and told the crowd, "These marbles are for today and tomorrow because I am here with you." There were murmurs and some tears among the audience.

As Mike closed his remarks, he poured all the marbles back into the jar and brought out another large bag and poured them into the jar as well. "I am a field leader at LegalShield," he said. "These are the days I get to enjoy with my daughter because I work from home and see my daughter every day!"

The crowd rose to their feet—many in tears, myself among them. The power of these leaders and this business was in such strong synergy with my family background. It joined my legal career and my love of network marketing, instilled by Ron Clark at Jafra. I had found a home. And I poured all my efforts into the success of these amazing people. It was more than a job. It was a calling. At our first event in Florida together, I told Mike I wanted to be present when he pulled the final marble from the jar.

Two years into my time running LegalShield, when I was living in Dallas, I received a text one evening that read, "Rip, it is Diana. I've moved to LA. Hope you are well. It would be nice to see you."

It was a pleasant surprise to hear from her. It was almost five years since we'd seen each other. I immediately fired back, "Diana, great to hear from you. Hope you are terrific. I sold my home in Beverly Hills several years ago, but it would be great to see you."

Three days later, I was in Los Angeles, staying at the Beverly Wilshire, waiting to see the lovely Diana. She was working as the chief of staff of Richard Riordan, the former mayor of Los Angeles. Earlier she had opened a medical packaging business that took off after it started.

When we saw each other that day at the hotel, we both felt an instant connection as we talked about the years lost and how we had been doing since our last encounter.

That meeting marked a new chapter in my life as Diana and I have been inseparable ever since. She is the love of my life. She treats my kids with love and kindness. Life gave me a second chance at happiness with Diana.

After the surprising departure of Mark Smith, the regional manager of California, in 2011, I initiated a series of visits and addresses by preeminent LegalShield leaders from around the country. Each of these leaders had large national organizations with a presence in the California market. Although the support of these leaders was invaluable, this market needed a full-time field leadership presence—a resident in the state.

I took time to consult with Darnell and other leaders, and I prepared a short list of exceptional candidates. My first choice was Larry and Doni Smith, who were serving as the regional managers in Arizona. Larry and I had become close friends during our immersion in the redesign of the LegalShield comp plan in 2011. I visited with him and Doni often at their home in Phoenix and enjoyed quiet dinners and often appeared together at large gatherings.

Diana's 50th birthday -
Beverly Hills, CA. 2014

In 2013, I invited Larry and Doni Smith to meet Diana and me at the St. Regis Hotel in Dana Point, CA, for dinner. They had been incredibly devoted to LegalShield. Larry and I are a day apart in age. He served two tours in Vietnam and was awarded the Bronze Star.

He was at a point in his career when he wanted to slow things down. Instead, I asked him to come on board as the regional leader of all operations in California. I needed him. The statewide operations needed him. He and Doni accepted, and I will be forever grateful. We became great friends.

Mike Humes and I appeared at many LegalShield events over the years since I heard him talk about his daughter and the jar of marbles. One day Mike called and said, "Next week, I am removing the final marble. Mikayla is turning 18 years old."

The event was being held in California in 2017, and Diana and I were going to be there for what promised to be an emotional moment. Unbeknownst to Mike, I arranged to fly Mikayla from

Maryland to surprise her dad as he pulled out the last marble. Darnell was Mikayla's godfather, and his son Malik is Mikayla's lifelong friend. Malik accompanied her on the flight and helped keep her hidden at the hotel. The evening Mikayla and Malik landed, Diana and I took Mike out to dinner.

I needed to keep him away from the hotel, and as always, we enjoyed a marvelous evening, filled with laughter and thoughts on the events that would unfold the next morning.

We woke up to a perfect Saturday morning in southern California. Diana and I met Mike for coffee, and as the event got underway, I texted with Malik. He brought Mikayla down and waited with her behind closed doors while the meeting was underway. I was brought to the stage and shared with the audience my reflections on the Orlando event years earlier. Mike came onstage and delivered an inspirational message. He brought out the jar of marbles and dumped out all of them except one. As he was reaching in to grasp the remaining marble, Mikayla appeared in the back of the ballroom and walked up the center aisle toward the stage.

Mike froze and stared. He was in disbelief. As Mikayla ascended the stage, they tearfully extracted the final marble as an emotionally charged audience cheered. Several months later, Mike was a father again with the arrival of his daughter Maia. I was honored to be asked by Mike to be her godfather.

I embarked on a series of field meetings that lasted for several years. Each week as my duties at the office came to a close, I headed to the airport for a different city, often meeting Dave Savula, Darnell, or Mike. I arranged international trips for the top leaders. We traveled to London, Rome, Rio, and other cities.

I spoke at the regional meetings and found a voice that brought me back to my dad, often using history as the backdrop to drive home the message of excellence and overcoming obstacles. One of my best-received addresses focused on an overview of justice and equality in America. I started with the Declaration of Independence and concluded with the Civil Rights Act of 1964. I mentioned my dad often and talked about our first drive to Florida together as a family during the 1950s' years of segregation.

Mike Humes and my goddaughter Maia - Maryland. 2020

I recalled my confusion at age six, at seeing a sign on the restroom that said, "Colored Only." My dad leaned down and placed his hand on my shoulder. Pointing to the Colored Only restroom, he calmly said, "Use that one, son."

In 2014, our annual convention was held at the MGM Grand in Las Vegas. The MGM has the largest arena within a hotel in the United States. Known as the Grand Garden Arena, it has hosted some of the finest entertainment in the world. We booked 3,000 rooms for LegalShield associates, and more than 14,000 were in attendance. In my opening, I quoted the Roman poet Horace from an ode written in 23 BC:

"Be wise. Decant the wine, and since our time is brief, cut back your far-reaching hope. For even while we talk, envious time has fled. Carpe diem—seize the day, put little trust in the future."

Chapter 9

Vermont and a Wedding

I first brought Diana to Vermont in the summer of 2015. We headed to Middlebury for the wedding of my college roommate's son Cully Cavness to his wife Emily. They were both graduates of Middlebury, and the wedding was held on the campus in Meade Chapel. Cully was awarded a Watson Fellowship upon graduation, and he attended the Oxford University Saïd Business School in Britain.

Emily was from a distinguished military family. Her dad and uncle wore full Marine dress at the service. Following the wedding, we joined the raucous wedding party at Tourterelle, a lovely French restaurant overlooking Lake Champlain. Diana and I strolled out on the lawns and enjoyed the view, with a glass of wine in hand. Emily's uncle approached us and after greetings, he inquired about LegalShield.

I shared with him my excitement about the company, the field leadership, and the service plans—sounding a bit like a proud parent. I paused, looked at him, and said, "Please tell me about your career."

He smiled. "I was a commander of two space shuttle missions."

The day after the wedding, Diana and I drove up the mountains to Goshen, Vermont, and to my favorite country inn, Blueberry Hill. Diana loved the charm of the inn, a place where cell phones, internet, or TV aren't allowed. She was immediately taken by Tony Clark, the proprietor and my close friend.

After checking into our room, we made a short drive down the gravel road turning on to Lady Slipper Lane—a private road. As we drove down the lane, she was delighted when I told her I had purchased land here in 1984 from Tony.

I parked the car, and we entered the deep woods encompassing the entire 86 acres of the land. As we walked among the pine, maple, oak, and birch trees, I shared with her the vision I had for this land when I was a young lawyer in the mid-1980s. That's when my brother Tom and my college friend Dave Sheldon and I were making our annual hikes on the Long Trail, traversing the peaks of the Green Mountains from the Vermont/Massachusetts line, north to the Canadian border. These summer adventures planted in me a long-held appreciation for the majesty of the Vermont mountains.

As we walked a short distance into the woods, I noticed that Diana was lingering behind me. As I turned, she was placing sticks on the forest floor as a guide back to the parked car. We both immediately erupted in laughter.

I told her about the small one-room log cabin I had once imagined building on the property, but we were quickly bound on a far more expansive venture. Diana's appreciation of the mountains was evident during our early-morning hikes on the Long Trail up Mt. Horrid from Brandon Gap.

Over the next several days, our plans grew as we imagined building a summer residence—a special gathering place for our family and friends. This expanded vision of the development of the land high up in the Green Mountains would require extensive planning. We were engaged by this time, but we had not decided where we would get married. Hosting our wedding at the new house would form an indelible connection with Vermont. I had embarked on several building projects in the past—and had promised myself I'd never to do it again—and I recommended that three years would give us more than enough time to pull it all together.

As a first step, we engaged the services of Avery Hamilton, a renowned architect. Avery had designed exceptional homes in

Vermont and in Greenwich, Connecticut. Avery shared our vision for a residence with strong local Vermont elements, and we settled on an updated version of the traditional yellow Vermont farmhouse, complete with a wraparound porch and cupola.

Throughout the rest of 2015 and 2016, I worked closely with Avery on the location for the house. Our Vermont neighbor, Steve Sherrill, provided great assistance on figuring out the best place for the home on the property, and he also introduced us to heavy equipment operators—who would play an essential role in starting to clear the homesite. Once we decided on a site for the house, I purchased federal topographic maps. Considering that the elevation was over 1,600 feet, my hope was the clearing to the west would include views across Lake Champlain to the Adirondack mountains in upstate New York. Local "experts" and loggers did not think this was likely.

Clearing forest land in Vermont requires a certification from a state-licensed forester that the area to be cleared does not include moose bedding areas or marshland. Most of the 10 acres we were clearing complied with the guidelines. The Lathrop brothers from Lincoln, VT, were highly regarded for their harvesting of trees and land clearance. Before they could bring their specialized logging rigs onto Lady Slipper Lane, we needed to do extensive improvements so the road could support and carry the weight.

In the summer of 2016, with approvals in hand, the Lathrops set to work. They harvested mature hardwood trees for lumber and flooring and ground up limbs and small trees for wood pellets that would be used in the heating furnaces in Burlington. As they worked their way toward the western boundary of the large clearing, the Adirondacks emerged into view. A positive omen for the multiyear project.

Wedding Lady Slipper Lane, VT. 2018

In Vermont, clearing trees is merely the first step in preparing forested land for building. Each stump would sprout innumerable shoots the next spring, and large excavation equipment must be brought in to pull out every stump, along with its roots. Jim Ploof and his son James and partner Toby were exceptional. Operating enormous bucket loaders, they meticulously dug out each stump and deposited them in large commercial dumpsters for removal.

With winter 2016–17 approaching and the stumps removed, Jim started rough grading for drainage. We also brought in a well-drilling rig and found plentiful cold and crystal-clear water at a depth of 650 feet. Finally, an engineer secured state approvals for a septic field design, which Jim installed before the snow started to fall.

As these efforts were underway, Avery and I were making the final plans for the house. Earlier he had introduced me to Matt Laberge, his preferred builder. Matt and his crew were well regarded and had constructed some of the finest homes in the state. He was known as a demanding craftsman. Matt was clearing his calendar for summer 2017, when he hoped to begin construction.

Diana and I began thinking the new house would easily be completed in time for the wedding at the end of August 2018. That proved not to be easy at all.

During the summer of 2017, Jim Ploof excavated the house site, installing drainage and more than three feet of crushed stone, where Matt and his crew poured the foundation slab and walls. Avery had specified concrete rather than block to provide an impervious moisture barrier. It was a race against winter's arrival to build the deck that covered the 10-foot-deep finished basement and the framing for the first, second, and third floors and the roof. With that framing completed, construction and mechanical systems installations could proceed during the long Vermont winter months. By late December, the framing was done and exterior doors and windows were delivered. Soon the house was closed in, and interior construction and mechanical systems installations could proceed during the long Vermont winter months. I was confident the project could be completed by end of July. -seven months away.

In the winter and early spring of 2018, Diana and I were living in Las Vegas, and I returned to Vermont every month during that time and stayed at Blueberry Hill for a week to 10 days each visit.

Vermont winters in the mountains are both beautiful and frigid. January 2018 proved exceptionally challenging. A large arctic air mass dropped temperatures to 20 below zero. Even with the dire cold, Matt and his team were on the job every day. Matt and I reviewed the construction schedule nearly daily. He was aware that Diana and I had set a date of August 25 for the wedding, and he was already becoming concerned about the timing. I authorized overtime for his crew and subcontractors, including on weekends.

In April, I moved into Blueberry Hill and was on the jobsite every morning by 5:00 a.m. Tom, one of Matt's senior crew members, arrived between 5:00 a.m. and 5:30 a.m. I brought coffee for him from the inn, and every morning we reviewed the progress from the prior day and the work plan for the one about to start.

As efforts on the site continued, two local cabinetmakers were fully engaged building the extensive cabinetry designed by Avery, with Diana's input. The house had six bathrooms, a large kitchen, and specialty cabinets on the first floor, which meant that more than eight master cabinetmakers were engaged for months.

After my early-morning site visits, I continued to hike the steep Long Trail pathway north to the summit of Mt Horrid. The isolation and exertion provided a calming break from the increasing time pressure of the construction and the approaching wedding day.

In late April, I invited Matt and his wife Judy to meet Diana and me for dinner. Matt had been putting in 18-hour days to complete the construction. After an enjoyable dinner, I invited them to our August wedding.

As Diana and I headed back to the inn, she pointed out that with guests and family arriving from across the country and a seated and plated dinner, space was limited in our great room. I responded that the best way to make sure the house was completed in time for the wedding was to have them invited. Diana smiled knowingly.

During the spring, back in Las Vegas, Diana and I were busy ordering kitchen supplies and other household items. The clerks and managers at the Williams Sonoma store in Summerlin got to know us by first name. We assembled an enormous variety of deliverables in our garage at Queensridge, including my Ducati motorcycle.

I had moved a number of times while I resided in Dallas, when I was operating LegalShield. That's when I met Jesse, the talented and trustworthy owner of an independent moving company. I still maintained a large storage unit in Dallas. In late spring 2018, I reached out to Jesse to arrange a cross-country collection of furniture and other belongings for delivery to the home in Goshen, VT. We settled on August 5 as a "safe" date.

Jesse and his crew drove their enormous moving van from Dallas to Las Vegas, and I flew from Vermont to meet them. Loading up the van, they headed to Dallas, and I met them late the following day. We emptied the storage unit and headed north to Vermont, and I met them at the house two days later. With barely three weeks until the wedding, the house was abuzz with painters, cabinetmakers, plumbers, and electricians.

Jesse completed his delivery. We still awaited the delivery of a number of antiques from Connecticut and new furniture, including outdoor teak furniture from Restoration Hardware in Summerlin, NV. Most of the furniture was stored in the large garage, awaiting completion of work inside the house.

Spending summers in the mountains would be remote, and we would be without access to the many entertainment choices available in Las Vegas. Diana and I enjoyed going to the movies on Sunday afternoons. Building the home in Goshen provided an interesting opportunity to bring the movies to us.

Las Vegas has many specialty-media equipment stores, and I visited the Magnolia store in Summerlin. This "store within a store" was located in the local Best Buy. I discovered that few Best Buy retail stores offer the high-end Magnolia equipment and service offerings. I was introduced to the manager of the Summerlin store, Kurt Baker, and told him about our Vermont project. Kurt confirmed that Vermont did not have any Magnolia stores, and I was impressed when he offered his assistance and the support of his team and engineers. We spent several hours reviewing the building plans, including the rough electrical design and ceiling heights.

Avery and I had designated the large room above the garage as the media room. The team in Summerlin and I reviewed a wide variety of state-of-the-art equipment, including a new Sony 4K projection system, which we selected.

When the house framing was completed, Kurt arranged to fly Arnold, his lead engineer, to Vermont to meet Matt and his carpenters, along with our electrician. Arnold led the efforts on the system design and installation in the media room (as well as other systems throughout the house). Several months later, Arnold arrived with precise and detailed wiring plans and a team of Magnolia staff arrived from their only store in New Hampshire to oversee every aspect of the installation.

As the interior finish work and painting were in full activity, Tammy Walsh and her team of talented landscapers were hard at work installing the extensive cut-stone patios and stone walls and walkways. Her crew was predominately female, and I referred to them as the Bangles, a tribute to the female rock band from the 1980s. Tammy enjoyed the designation. She and her partner Fran became dear friends and regular visitors.

Also underway was the installation and seeding of our vast 10-acre lawn. Jim Ploof arranged a visit by Pete, the owner of Green Haven Nursery in Essex Junction, Vermont.

I met with Jim and Pete on the site, and Pete asked, "What do you have in mind?"

Looking out on the mountains, with the Adirondacks distant, I said I wanted a lush, weed-free lawn. He chuckled because he knew growing grass like that would be nearly impossible on the top of a mountain with rock under the entire cleared area. He volunteered that as far as he knew, it had never been done in Vermont. We quickly started discussing how it could be accomplished, and the only solution was to truck in sufficient sandy subsoil to provide a one-foot-thick cover and then truck in fertile topsoil to provide another six inches to support the lawn growth and depth of grass roots.

Lady Slipper Lane Goshen,VT. 2021

"How many commercial truckloads do you think are required?" I asked.

Pete and Jim's response: "At least a thousand."

Truckloads began arriving before dawn seven days a week, and they made multiple trips after dark. After a month of deliveries, with Jim and his crew grading the new soil, in July it was ready to hydro seed. A little more than a month before the wedding, I was assured the grass would germinate in time. Turf would be trucked in from Maine for installation around the large stone patio, where the outdoor wedding service would be held.

Of course, obstacles intervened. Summer 2018 was one of the driest on record. The newly hydro-seeded areas needed water, but with no rain forecasted, Pete brought in enormous tanker trucks that took water from nearby streams. That was halted when they were intercepted by state officials. We ended up sourcing water commercially at great expense.

Ten days before the wedding, the turf arrived and was installed with large rollers adjacent to the patios and in the front of the house. Jim Ploof was finishing up the driveway, which I designed as a grassy circle directly in front of the entrance door. Jim's son James assisted me. I had found two large boulders on Lady Slipper Lane to place in the middle of the circle. One boulder was larger than the other. Even with his large Cat excavator, James could not lift the rocks. He rolled them across the lane and down the driveway to the house, placing them deftly. One boulder had an indentation, the other a slight curve. I asked James to position them with the curve of the smaller stone nestled into the indentation of the larger one.

As James waited on the excavator, I went inside the house, which was alive with installers and painters. I asked Diana to come outside to look at the boulders. She smiled and noted how nice they looked. A moment later, she turned to me with tears and exclaimed, "That's us!" Glancing out at James, I noticed that he felt the emotion of the moment. Trying to hide his own tears, he offered, "That's the most amazing thing I've ever seen."

Diana had prepared a wedding website that included schedules, local activities, and attractions. We planned a barbecue at the house on August 23rd and invited the wedding guests and all the contractors that had worked on the construction to come with their spouses or partners. We booked the entire Blueberry Hill Inn to lodge our guests. All our kids, along with John and Darcy Hoffman and my sister Karen, stayed with us at our house in the newly completed bedrooms.

Earlier that spring, Karen gave Diana our mom's wedding dress. Worn only once at my parents' wedding in September 1950, the dress was deposited unceremoniously in a plastic bag. Diana was overcome by Karen's generosity and the gesture. Their friendship and affection have become a lovely part of our family life.

They took the dress out of the bag and saw right away that it had been damaged by the years. Large yellow stains had formed on the fabric. It appeared to be irretrievably damaged. They quickly conceived the idea of taking a cutting from Mom's dress and incorporating it into Diana's. First Diana sent the dress to our cleaning service in Las Vegas and asked them to remove a section and try to clean it. The owner asked, "How soon do you need this?"

The wedding was still some months away, and he asked if he could have some time to try several cleaning methods. Diana immediately approved, and the dress was delivered nearly two months later.

Diana called and asked me to come home. I walked into our condo and found her there wearing my mom's dress. It was perfectly white without a hint of any stains. Amazingly, it fit her perfectly and didn't need any tailoring. We felt the power and emotion of the moment. No words needed to convey the magic and presence of my mom.

Diana and I finally began living in the house just a week before the wedding, even while last-minute efforts were underway to make the home wedding ready. On the morning of August 23rd, Matt and several of his carpenters arrived. The screens for the porch had been completed and needed to be installed and painted before the barbecue.

With less than two hours to go before the guests arrived, I walked out and announced, "Time's up!"

Everyone laughed at the final-hour readiness. They all returned later, with wives and girlfriends, ready to share their efforts and results with their families and our wedding guests. Delivery and completion could have not been more down to the final moment.

As part of the wedding surprise, Diana enlisted me to do a short dance with her. I agreed to this only if I could select the music. I settled on "Brass in Pocket," a bluesy 1979 release by the Pretenders. Diana arranged for a choreographer from Las Vegas to work with us and develop the routine. He had worked with a number of Vegas entertainers and had designed performances for Cirque du Soleil. For our first meeting, we exchanged ideas, and he played the song in his studio and asked us to dance.

Diana is an exceptional dancer and for a number of years competed in ballroom dancing. The choreographer smiled as she glided effortlessly across the dance floor. Next it was my turn, and feeling a bit cocky, I put on my best "aren't-I-cool" moves. He instantly asked me to stop and came over to the two of us and looked at me.

"Here's the way you have to think about this," he said. "She's the picture. You're just the frame." I understood immediately.

At our condo, Diana used painter's tape to create the space in the screened-in porch at the house in Goshen where we would perform after the wedding dinner. That's where we practiced.

We asked our wonderful friend John Hoffman, whom I had worked with at LegalShield, to officiate at the wedding. John was an ordained minister. His wife Darcy and Diana had become very close friends and confidants.

As the wedding day arrived, we hosted a prewedding reception with great food and champagne for the guests. Diana, in the first of the four dresses she wore that evening, joined us for an hour as we mingled and as the photographer chronicled the evening.

Diana left the gathering along with Darcy and her cousin Sharon to get into her wedding dress. A short while later, John asked the guests to be seated. The kids and I were on the covered porch that faces west. The guests seated in front of us faced the Adirondacks.

After a quiet moment, the DJ played, "Somewhere Over the Rainbow," as sung by Eva Cassidy, in an emotional treatment of the classic song from The Wizard of Oz. After several verses, the kids and I in a line walked up the aisle holding hands. Charlotte and Taylor were to my right and Diana's kids, Kennedy and Colin, were to my left.

For the final verse, the boys exchanged places, and Colin was holding Charlotte's hand while Taylor gripped Kennedy's. The circle and family were now complete. We were one.

Opening the service, John noted that "Somewhere Over the Rainbow" was my mom's favorite song. Taylor sang it many years earlier at the close of her memorial service.

As the crowd sat quietly absorbing the view and the moment, the kids and I all put on sunglasses. I motioned to the DJ to "hit it, Patrick!"

The pounding sounds of "Something Just Like This" by Coldplay and the Chainsmokers started, and as the first verse ended, I walked back toward the porch. When it once again reached the phrase, "Something just like this," the French doors swung open, and I offered my hand to Diana from the steps. As she descended to the patio, we started to dance and the guests stood up, smiling and dancing with us.

The wedding was wonderful—terrific food, great wine, and a series of toasts. The most moving and memorable was offered by Taylor, who recounted our days together with Charlotte and his love of our family. A number of tissues appeared around the room.

After the wedding, a quiet descended as Diana and I enjoyed the peaceful close of the summer. Fall arrived early in the mountains, and by mid-September, the early-morning temperatures slipped into the 30s, with frost appearing on the ground. The hot weather of the summer was forgotten as we turned on the radiant heat in the house for the first time and built occasional fires in the fireplaces.

We continued our early-morning hikes up Mt. Horrid and were invigorated by the crisp, clean air. Diana grew up in Alabama, and she had never seen the fall foliage colors of the northeast. She was amazed as the leaves changed, and she took videos as we drove up Lady Slipper Lane. In early October, with the leaves at their peak color, we returned to Vegas with plans to come back to Goshen for the Thanksgiving and Christmas holidays—our first in our new mountain home. Kennedy was with us when we returned a few days before Thanksgiving to prepare the traditional dinner. My brother Tom and his wife Emily were joining us, along with my sister Karen. Thanksgiving was unusually cold with morning temps as low as four degrees. Nearly a foot of fresh snow fell a few days before Thanksgiving. Diana, Kennedy, and I went sledding while Tom and Emily went cross-country skiing around the large snow-covered lawn. Great fun!

Kennedy was attending the Hun School in Princeton, and after we drove her back for classes, Diana and I again enjoyed the quiet and started early plans for Christmas. In mid-December, I cut down a Christmas tree at our neighbor's home and dragged it back to the house and put it up in our great room. The smell of fresh-cut pine while the tree was decorated was the harbinger for a real "first Christmas" on the mountain.

On December 22, with Kennedy back from classes, we invited several neighbors to join us for an Italian dinner and a movie in the newly completed media room. The day had started with cold temperatures in the single digits, but by late afternoon, before our guests arrived, it was much warmer. When the movie finished at 9:30 p.m., we walked our friends to the front door and saw that it was now raining hard, with temperatures in the mid-50s.

A front was expected overnight with bitter cold forecast for the next day. Diana and I shared a quiet moment looking at the Christmas tree and headed to bed.

The pounding rain continued throughout the night, but it abruptly stopped at 4:16 a.m., followed by a blinding flash of lightning and a simultaneous explosion that rocked the house. I felt the concussion deep in my chest. Diana was instantly awake and leapt out of bed to check on Kennedy. I tried the bedroom lights and picked up the phones I had just purchased that afternoon. Nothing. I tried to process what was happening and realized that the new generator was already installed and tested, and the electricity should have been on.

I pulled on a coat as I ran down the stairs and exited the garage door out the back—immediately tripping on unseen sharp objects all over the patio. Returning briefly to the kitchen, I picked up a flashlight. An enormous crater had formed in the patio directly under our bedroom window, less than six feet from the side of the house.

I knew instantly that we had been hit by lightning. There had been no lightning or thunder all night, and this strike was a singular event. The temperature had dropped below freezing in moments. I inspected the area around the strike and found pieces of the patio peppered into the north side of the house, which was completely covered in mud. The force of the strike had peeled back the sod that had been installed there in August.

With the temperature continuing to drop and without power, I needed to get in touch with the power company as soon as possible. With the numbers near zero by morning, the water lines could freeze. All lines of communications were knocked out, so I jumped in my car and headed south to a crossroad where there was a small window of cell coverage. In moments I reached the power company, and a dispatcher said they were aware of the outage and crews were on the way. Back at the house, Diana and Kennedy were shaken up. The violence of the proximate lightning strike was profound. A short while later, I saw the lights of two power trucks heading down the lane and ran out to meet them. They said a lightning strike had hit a mile away at the Blueberry Hill Inn and all the transformers between the inn and our house had been destroyed.

"The lightning hit right here," I said, correcting them. "Next to my house."

They were perplexed and followed me behind the house with their large, commercial flashlights. They couldn't believe what they saw as they illuminated the scene.

"I've been doing this for over 25 years," one of them said. "I've never seen anything like this."

They were immediately worried about fire danger. "Have you checked your basement. Your wiring could be burning from the impact."

They were prohibited from entering homes, but in light of this destruction, they could take a look with me. As we walked down to the basement, we didn't smell smoke or burning. They inspected our circuit panels, and both appeared to be intact.

They were aware that the dropping temperature could lead to further damage and promised to work quickly and replace the multiple transformers all the way back to Blueberry Hill. They promised not to leave until the power was restored.

I went through the house. The water was not working, and I called the well driller and woke him up. I called Matt Laberge. He and his family were in Florida, but two members of his crew and Jody, his electrician, arrived at the house within an hour and a half as the sun was coming up.

The well driller arrived shortly after and concluded that the new well pump and electronics were destroyed. He began replacing all of it. Soon the power came on, and we discovered that the heating system had survived the blast.

In the early-morning light, we surveyed the damage. The lightning had followed a metal barrier strip that went along the patio to the other side of the house and had exited and struck a tree. We saw a series of deep gashes where it had traversed the lawn to strike the tree. The screens on the north-facing side of the screened-in porch were blown out. There was mud, rock, and grass imbedded in the ceiling and in the ceiling of the wraparound porch. The north-facing siding was destroyed, along with the eaves at the roof line.

A growing group of carpenters and electricians could not believe the damage and our good fortune that the shrapnel from the patio explosion did not injure us in our bed just a few feet away.

I drove back up the road to the location where I could get cell service connection and called the insurance carrier. They were exceptional and promised to provide any assistance required. I declined their inquiry about whether we wanted to temporarily relocate.

I didn't know at the time that the new generator, security systems, cameras, and all the state-of-the-art media equipment— including the speakers—were totally destroyed.

Life up in the Green Mountains was off the grid. We enjoyed national forest land on the north and south boundaries of the property, and to the north there was no buildings for more than four and a half miles from our home.

After my career in some of the world's major cities, I enjoyed the serenity, quiet, and deep-black nights—without light pollution. On a clear night it was amazing to see millions of stars twinkling brightly and to go to sleep with the night sounds of the nearby woods.

The isolation did come with some interesting challenges. For one, there was no cell service, and as I continued my career, having internet and cell access was essential. I had seen television ads for a local satellite internet service, and I was confident an easy solution could be found. They installed a dish, and soon we were back up and online, in a fashion. Unfortunately, the promised "high-speed" solution was not so fast. With a maximum download capability of 25 Mbps, time delays were frequent and streaming was not possible. Upload speeds were even worse at 5 Mbps. Within a month, I knew we needed a better solution.

I contacted the local cable company to inquire about a high-speed fiber-optic cable connection. I gave them our address, and they said no service was available where we were. The closest node was more than four miles distant. I asked for a quote to run the line to the house, and they laughed in disbelief.

"We've never run a dedicated line that far to service a single residence," they said.

I told them I was serious, and an hour later, an executive from their commercial division called me and arranged to visit our location the next week with his lead engineers and installers.

Several weeks later, after confirming that installing a four-and-a-half-mile fiber-optic line was possible, they returned with a proposal. They would run a commercial-grade encrypted line at bank and federal-office standards, delivering at minimum 200 Mbps synchronous speed. This would provide the same speed for downloads and uploads of data. The speed could be pushed up to a Gig if requested. The installation would take six months. Absorbing sticker shock at the project pricing, I agreed. The work was done throughout the winter and was complete by spring 2019.

Returning to Goshen, I held my breath as they completed the connection. Success! The speeds, as promised, were exceptional, and the stable Wi-Fi also supported our security monitoring and provided access to the Nest thermostats and cameras throughout the interior and exterior of the house. We also no longer had a problem enabling voice over Wi-Fi on our phones' cell service.

I was back in business.

The new high-speed connection offered several other unanticipated benefits. I was able to access the Vermont camera settings while sitting comfortably in our living room in Las Vegas. I had the media team install a large camera facing west at the eave of the roof. It had exceptional optics, and I could zoom in as well as move the camera from my phone with the touch of a finger. On many a winter evening, Diana and I sat quietly at our home in Las Vegas, watching the snow fall in Vermont from thousands of miles away.

In early 2019, I was contacted by my friend Jesse Watson, the founder of Virgo, a private equity fund in San Francisco. Jesse had been a new executive at CD&R when I was running Jafra Cosmetics, and he and I first worked together then, nearly twenty years earlier.

Jesse asked me to attend a meeting with him in San Francisco with his Virgo partners and several executives from their portfolio companies. The meeting was well organized, and I was impressed with the company overviews presented by several of their operating executives. At the end of the day, and before a reception and dinner, Jesse asked me to make some remarks about private equity from my perspective of having managed six portfolio companies.

The atmosphere was relaxed, and I began by complimenting the presenting executives. Many of them were new to private equity company management. I noted the differences depending upon the business variations and pointed out the common aspects they should keep in mind. "Private equity is the tip of the spear," I said. "Interest rates are nearly zero. Institutional investors, including insurance companies, large college endowments, and pension funds, look to private equity investment to spike their returns. Rarely do they allocate more than ten percent of their funds, but they expect an outsized return. Complete management focus and urgency is essential. Management rewards are exceptional and based exclusively on expected success. "Think about it this way," I continued. "In essence, you're much like an NFL or NBA coach. You're here because of your prior success. Your first year should be dedicated to building your team. Develop a deep understanding of all facets of your business. Develop a fully analyzed strategic plan to grow your business and contain expenses. Based on that, build out a tactical plan. Success is predicated on execution, not on strategy. Forget about weekends or holidays.

"In your second year, it's expected that your results will improve dramatically. In essence, that you will make the playoffs. In year three, you should win the Super Bowl or the NBA Finals. If not— you're gone. Scores of new coaches will be ready to take your seat."

I glanced at Jesse, and he was all smiles. Many of the execs enjoyed the sports analogy—absorbing the sense of urgency. Others appeared a bit panicked. Several of them approached me with more questions at the reception and the dinner.

Jesse called a few weeks later and asked if I would be interested in joining him on the board of directors of ARM, an interesting business majority owned by Virgo. ARM provided crop loans to farmers, primarily in the states along the Mississippi River.

When I agreed to serve on the board, I received volumes of financial and operational data and attended my first board meeting in Denver in August 2019. The business model was interesting. The crop loans were supported by federal crop insurance. Accordingly, loan losses were minimal.

After my first board meeting, Jesse called and asked, "Would you like to take over as CEO?"

We laughed as I observed, "Those days are behind me. It's time to have a life."

I did agree to work closely as an adviser to Virgo and the management team, noting that I had an idea for a candidate to serve as a new CEO.

As I continued to engage with Virgo and the management of ARM, I discovered multiple opportunities and a host of necessary course corrections. For the rest of 2019 and into 2020, I worked closely with Scott Guthrie—a former executive at Disney and a Virgo partner. Scott and I hit it off immediately, recognizing that we'd had similar areas of focus.

I knew Virgo was intent on changing its executive management, and I had determined early on that issues at ARM were related more to revenue rather than expenses, which largely seemed controlled. As the end of the year approached, schisms became apparent among the current executive ranks. The company required a new CEO with proven people skills and team-building instincts.

Among the other problems management had left unaddressed were fundamental issues, including a clear bonus program to incentivize local managers and corporate staff. A granular operational review was required. The singular loan facility offered to farmers failed to provide opportunities to engage a broad spectrum of the farm community as it was centered on lower-credit-qualified operations. This resulted in questions within the farming industry about what the company was.

I brought in Jerry Thomas at Decision Analyst in Dallas. They had provided exceptional research for us at LegalShield. I also secured my great friend and business partner Alan Fearnley to work with me for the seventh time. Jesse also knew Alan well from our days together at Jafra.

Alan and Jerry produced an outstanding 150-page report of detailed information and marketing analysis. Though much of the findings were confirmatory, they revealed several "aha" revelations, including that much of the company business was secured predominantly from third parties rather than via prospecting generally by the local area managers.

In February 2020, Diana and I were enjoying our annual midwinter visit to Cabo San Lucas, Mexico, when we started hearing news about the rapid global expansion of Covid-19 infections. I called United Airlines, concerned that potential border closures could leave us stranded. No US flights from Mexico were affected, and we returned to Las Vegas.

Kennedy was a junior at the Hun School in Princeton. She played basketball in the winter, and she was a rower on the crew team. In early March, during the first week of spring break, the team traveled to Clemson University in South Carolina for practices. Diana was meeting Kennedy in Clemson, and for the second week of vacation, they planned to visit several southern schools that were attempting to recruit Kennedy to play basketball. They toured several universities but began receiving notices that the others were closing for the remainder of the school year due to Covid. In days, businesses across the country went into lockdown. Diana and Kennedy returned to Las Vegas.

The outlook was dire. Covid-related deaths were accelerating everywhere. Food shortages developed as families in fear began to hoard food. Grocery store shelves were empty of basic goods, foods, and supplies. At the time, there was no speculation about when the crisis might end, and we decided that Goshen was a better location to ride out the pandemic. The Hun School was planning remote learning, and a move to Vermont would put Kennedy on the east, in the same time zone.

On March 20, just three days after Diana and Kennedy returned from the east coast, I drove them to the Las Vegas airport. I remained behind because of several deliveries pending arrival and booked a flight for March 25. Travel from Vegas to Vermont required flight transfers in Chicago or Newark, and I arranged to have our neighbor Steve Sherrill meet Diana and Kennedy at the Burlington airport.

A day before my flights, I contacted Michael, our driver in Las Vegas, and asked him to pick me up at 3:30 a.m. to get me to the airport for the first United flight of the day to Newark. He confirmed the plans. The next morning at 3:30 a.m., I was called and told that Michael had arrived. I headed down the elevator and saw a new Mercedes was waiting. Michael Bandy, who cut my hair, opened the door to the car.

"Michael, what are you doing here?" I asked.

"I received your text yesterday," he responded, "and assumed you were stuck. I'm taking you to the airport."

We laughed about the mistaken contact and text, and I expressed my gratitude at his friendship and concern.

The Vegas airport seemed surreal—the normally teeming terminals were empty. I walked alone over the land bridge above the enormous baggage-claim area. This area is the size of two NFL football fields, and not a single person was there. I was the only passenger going through the extensive TSA screening, and I boarded the flight with only five passengers.

When we landed in Newark a few hours later, my phone alerts went off. My United connection to Burlington had been canceled, and I had been booked on a later flight. Below that was another alert that the later flight had also been canceled. I located a United rep who said it was likely that the flights the next day would be canceled as well. No one was traveling.

I called Hertz and picked up the last car in their inventory for the five-and-a-half-hour drive to Goshen. I called Diana and gave her an update. She told me she was feeling very ill. She had a severe headache, sore throat, and was experiencing body aches. She called Sean Ameli, our doctor in Las Vegas, and he was immediately concerned that she had caught Covid on the flights five days earlier. He wanted her in total isolation. The spread of the disease was not yet well understood, and he wanted her in quarantine for 21 days. He wasn't convinced that the recommended 14-day isolation was sufficient.

I did not see Diana for the next 21 days, except when I went outside and waved up to her at our bedroom window. I cooked all our meals while Kennedy was my "runner," taking plates upstairs for Diana, knocking on the door, and leaving the tray for her mom. I went to the grocery store for us once a week—going alone, quickly stocking up, and leaving.

Diana's quarantine was finished in mid-April, and we enjoyed a joyous reunion.

As Covid led to increasing shutdowns, Taylor and Charlotte, who were both living in New York, received notices that their employers were suspending operations. On the west coast, Diana's son Colin was also out of work.

Dramatic efforts were underway to contain the virus, but the spread continued unabated. In spring 2020, hopes for vaccines appeared to be several years' distant. We encouraged all our kids to join us in Vermont to ride it out together.

One of the unexpected pleasures of that year were the repeated visits by Taylor and Charlotte. I rented cars from Hertz, and Char picked up one just a block from her apartment. She and Taylor joined us for extended stays, and we cooked terrific dinners, watched movies, and enjoyed the time together. They came to love the house and the surrounding mountains, which were a dramatic counterpoint to life in the city.

Each morning I continued my ascent up the steep climb of Mt. Horrid, hiking for well more than 100 days each year.

Although businesses across the country closed down, farming operations continued as a lifeline to feed the nation. At ARM, we continued holding weekly calls, and like so many, we began using the new face-to-face offering of Zoom. This created a semblance of normalcy. In the summer of 2022, as I was continuing my early-morning ascent of Mt. Horrid on the Long Trail, it occurred to me that I was approaching a milestone. This climb, which starts at Brandon Gap, was first climbed by Tom, Dave Shelton, and me in 1982—40 years ago. It is a rigorous, 700-vertical-foot hike to the summit of the Great Cliffs, with one of the most outstanding views along the Long Trail.

To the east are the White Mountains of New Hampshire, and to the west are the Adirondacks of New York.

Twenty Twenty-Two was my fifth summer of more than 100 annual ascents. I realized that the original 272-mile, end-to-end journey in the early 1980s, from the Massachusetts-Vermont state line to Canada, coupled with more than 150 miles on the round-trip morning hikes up Mt. Horrid, totaled a thousand miles of hiking on the Long Trail.

In celebration, Dave Shelton flew up from Florida. He, Diana, and I ascended Mt. Horrid together. We wore commemorative Vermont green T-shirts. The front displayed "LT 1000" in white lettering, and on the right, it carried "'81 – '22."

My early-morning climbs continue. Many more miles await.

Our Goshen home has now become the family gathering place. All the kids return each summer, and the house is filled with laughter and the smells of great food.

I'm certain it's not possible for more abundant happiness to exist.

Reminiscence

In memory of friends who departed far too soon. Doug Grau, Gavin Cullen, Biff Bartley, Paul and Peter Fischer, Van Ottinger, Frank Ryan, Dave and Bev Savula, and Ken Taylor.

Tribute to Ken Taylor

Ambassador Kenneth Taylor died on October 15, 2015, following a two-month battle with colon cancer. One week before his death, I flew to New York and spent the day with Ken at the New York-Presbyterian Hospital. Of course, Ken had the finest room with expansive views of the East River and upper Manhattan.

We relived our many wonderful trips together. There was abundant laughter as we recounted having dinner several years earlier with Pat at La Grenouille in New York, one of Ken's favorites. During the course of the evening, Ken asked me about my upcoming travel. I responded that I was departing the next morning on the flight to London. Several hours later, while I was waiting at the airport gate, Ken and Pat strolled in.

Together we enjoyed the flight and several glasses of champagne. We also reminisced about many stories and laughed heartily about the day my young son Taylor took Ken to his third-grade class in Montecito and offered Ken for his show-and-tell.

As I departed Ken's hospital room late in the afternoon, he and I said our goodbyes. We were both tearful.

After our time together, I returned home to California, and Ken called the next evening with a request. "Rip, would you make some remarks at my memorial service?" he asked.

"Of course. I would be honored, Ken."

In closing and saying farewell for the final time, Ken offered, "Keep it light and feel free to make something up."

Several days later, when I was in Rome, Ken passed away. His son Douglas, a close friend, kept me apprised of the plans for the memorial service, and I flew to Toronto the evening before. The memorial was held at the cathedral in Toronto. The Royal Canadian Mounties, in their brilliant scarlet uniforms, were on horseback in front of the church. The cathedral was filled with several thousand people in attendance, including Canadian prime minister Justin Trudeau and his wife. A large contingent of the diplomatic community, Canadians, Americans, and representatives of other nations, were also there. The service was broadcast live throughout Canada.

Several close friends were invited to speak, and I was one of the two Americans. The mood was somber and reverential. I began my remarks by remembering Ken's admonition to "keep it light and feel free to make something up." The heaviness in the audience abated a bit.

"Let me address the elephant in the room," I announced. "Argo." There was laughter.

"The producers have contacted me after learning of Ken's passing. As the true story now comes to light, it happens that Ben Affleck was originally cast to play the role of Ken Taylor. As filming was approaching, the producers decided that Ben was neither good-looking enough nor cool enough to play the role of Ken Taylor."

Farewell, my friend

Vermont and a Wedding

Acknowledgments

Over the years, close friends and my wife Diana have suggested that the stories in this book should be shared. Setting out to memorialize a lifetime of experiences appeared relatively easy as an abstract concept. The execution was something else altogether. In the winter of 2021, with my 70th birthday looming in August, I knew it was time. Several important people have influenced my life and opportunities. They include my dad, my grandfather, Leigh Harris ("Pappy"), and my friends Ron Clark and Ambassador Ken Taylor. Though most of these men never knew one another, when I look back, I see that they shared aspects in their personalities and approaches to life.

They were all extremely smart and had an ability to laugh easily, and they never took themselves too seriously despite their exceptional success. Most important, they all provided quiet guidance only when asked. They gave me the space to fail without criticism. They believed in me even during times when I was less convinced of my abilities or judgment. Their stories and the impact they had on my life have been indelible and deserve to be shared.

Equally important were the love of my mom and the unwavering friendship of my brother Tom, my sister Karen, cousin Jeff, Dave Sheldon, Steve Bachelder, and college roommate Charles Cavness.

I also thank Henry Ferris for helping me with the editing of the book, and Zachariah Mattheus and Diane Aronson for their help in producing it.

Vermont and a Wedding

Accolades

"Rip Mason's *Carpe Diem* is a meditation in motion—a lucid, unpretentious memoir that maps a life of cultivated resolve and accidental grandeur. Rarely do recollections feel this lived-in, this quietly momentous. Mason does not mythologize; he records. And in doing so, he renders ambition not heroic, but human."

—*Guy Trebay*, Author and Award-Winning Columnist for The New York Times

"Rip Mason writes with the kind of clarity that bypasses ego and speaks straight to the human core. *Carpe Diem* is a compass for purposeful living, gently reminding us that integrity, grace, and quiet courage are still the most radical choices we can make."

—*Tiffany Hawk*, author of *Love Me Anyway*

"*Carpe Diem* is an unvarnished account of leadership shaped by conscience, not ambition. Rip Mason offers a rare look into the quiet architecture of influence where family, ethics, and restraint guide decision-making. In a time of noise and self-mythology, his story stands apart: lucid, dignified, and grounded in the deeper work of living a consequential life."

—*Steve Coll*, two-time Pulitzer Prize-winning journalist

"*Carpe Diem* begins with gentle melodies, then soars like a synth riff that resonates deep and wide. It stirs curiosity, leaves you fulfilled, and fills you with hope. It propels you to discover what is beyond the horizon, toward something profoundly meaningful."

— *Richard Flanagan*, Author and Man Booker Prize Winner

"Rip's tireless efforts and vast creativity to improve businesses for the benefit of all stakeholders is a constant theme in his management style. A natural collaborator, Rip was always guided by ethics and fairness that encouraged his teams and partners to share ideas and work together to drive successful outcomes. You will enjoy this book and share the journey together with Rip."

—*David Novak*, **President of Clayton Dubilier &Rice**

"Rip was a transformative CEO for our investment group at Legal Shield. Rip and the team at Legal Shield have helped bring quality legal services to all Americans. His strong knowledge of the direct selling business along with his authentic desire to help others made him a perfect leader to transition the business from the company's founder and to reposition the company for sustainable growth."

—*Ted Virtue*, **Founder and CEO of MidOcean Partners**

"I've worked with Rip for more than 20 years. His work ethic, consensus management, sense of urgency and focus on success inspires employees. Rip's dedication to family, formed in his early years, informs his worldview, and that, combined with consistent achievement of excellence, has resulted in a series of successful businesses. You will enjoy this book and indeed be moved."

—*Jesse Watson*, **Founder and CEO of Virgo Investment Group**

www.ingramcontent.com/pod-product-compliance
Lightning Source LLC
Chambersburg PA
CBHW051140120626
46547CB00012B/880